FIERCE
WOMAN

About the Author

Rhoda Shapiro has worked for a decade as a tantric educator, training women to step into their power by way of meditation, movement, dance, expression, and yoga. She has facilitated women's circles and taught workshops throughout Los Angeles and in the San Francisco Bay Area. Rhoda's YouTube channel, which has amassed thousands of subscribers, features yogic practices to empower viewers. Rhoda is also the founder/editor-in-chief of *The Milpitas Beat*, a Silicon Valley–based newspaper. She lives in the Bay Area with her husband, Eric, and their two sons. *Fierce Woman: Wake Up Your Badass Self* is her first book.

RHODA SHAPIRO

FIERCE WOMAN

wake up your
BADASS SELF

Llewellyn Publications
Woodbury, Minnesota

FIRST EDITION
First Printing, 2019

Book design: Samantha Penn
Cover design: Shira Atakpu
Editing: Annie Burdick

Llewellyn Publications is a registered trademark of Llewellyn Worldwide Ltd.

Library of Congress Cataloging-in-Publication Data
Names: Shapiro, Rhoda, author.
Title: Fierce woman : wake up your badass self / by Rhoda Shapiro.
Description: First edition. | Woodbury, Minnesota : Llewellyn Worldwide,
    2019.
Identifiers: LCCN 2019016693 (print) | LCCN 2019021526 (ebook) | ISBN
    9780738761022 (ebook) | ISBN 9780738760926
Subjects: LCSH: Self-acceptance. | Self-realization in women.
Classification: LCC BF575.S37 (ebook) | LCC BF575.S37 S455 2019
    (print) | DDC 158.1082—dc23
LC record available at https://lccn.loc.gov/2019016693

Llewellyn Worldwide Ltd. does not participate in, endorse, or have any authority or responsibility concerning private business transactions between our authors and the public.

All mail addressed to the author is forwarded, but the publisher cannot, unless specifically instructed by the author, give out an address or phone number.

Any internet references contained in this work are current at publication time, but the publisher cannot guarantee that a specific location will continue to be maintained. Please refer to the publisher's website for links to authors' websites and other sources.

Llewellyn Publications
A Division of Llewellyn Worldwide Ltd.
2143 Wooddale Drive
Woodbury, MN 55125.2989
www.llewellyn.com

Printed in the United States of America

This book is dedicated to all women.
May you remember the wonder of what you are
so that you set the world on fire with your light.

CONTENTS

SECTION I: MIND

SECTION II: BODY

SECTION III: HEART

SECTION IV: SPIRIT

POWER EXERCISES AND RITUALS

—————

POWER TIPS AND AFFIRMATIONS

DISCLAIMER

The author and publisher of this work assume no liability whatsoever for any injuries, issues, or harm experienced by the reader following, during, or surrounding the reading of this work. No information or advice in these pages is intended to substitute the guidance or care of a licensed medical professional. The author is not a licensed medical professional and makes no claim of being one. Any readers of this work in search of help for medical issues, both physical and psychological, are advised to pursue the care of a licensed medical professional.

ACKNOWLEDGMENTS

I want to start out by acknowledging my husband, Eric. Without him, the writing of this book would not have been possible. After dreaming about writing this book for months, I asked my husband what he thought about me putting all of my work on hold in order to bring my vision to life. Without a moment of hesitation, he told me to do it; within days, I started writing *Fierce Woman*. It took almost half the year. And in that time, Eric held it down, working like a madman to sustain our household, just so I could have the space to fully immerse myself in the creative process. So: a huge thank you to my husband for being one of the most supportive, creative, honest, and encouraging people I know.

Thank you to the team at Llewellyn Worldwide. I am forever in your debt. Your publishing company is a force of nature, and to be aligned with it is an absolute dream for me. Thank you to the amazing Elysia Gallo for opening this door of opportunity, and to the brilliant Heather Greene for all your guidance and dedication. And endless gratitude to powerhouse editor Annie Burdick for giving my book such love and care.

And thank you to Tanya Paluso for writing the book's foreword, and for all the beautiful work you do to pave the way for so many women.

I also want to thank all of the women who journeyed with me on the first virtual Feminine Power Circle that I started back in 2015. You women don't know this, but I was so inspired by working with all of you, and so honored to be your guide during our circle together, that the idea for this book started formulating in my body, mind, and heart. Thank you for entrusting me with all of your stories and your truth. To witness all of you stepping into your power was so humbling.

And I want to thank some of my dearest fierce women friends, whom I cherish so much. Jessika, Rachael, Naomi, Nicole, Jackee, Jette, Flo, Cerris, Jennifer, Jae, Ute, Eva, Rosemary… through different phases of my life, all of you have contributed so much to my journey, and have taught me the value of sisterhood and friendship.

And thank you to all of the strong women that I am fortunate enough to be able to call family: my Aunt Anna; my niece, Julia; my mother-in-law, Nita; my sister-in-law, Stephanie…and there are so many more.

Thank you also to my sister, Phyllis, who is such a source of inspiration each day.

And thank you to my mom for giving me strength, love, and, of course, life.

Finally, thank you to my dad, whom I miss every day, and whose strong presence I felt with me as I navigated the creative process.

FOREWORD

One of the most powerful rituals I use in my work is called the beam—when we hold up our hands to acknowledge what a woman has just shared. Usually, the women who've never experienced it before all have the same reaction.

They jump back in their seat, startled by the power of the energy coming at them. Having such a hard time receiving it, they usually put their hands up to deflect the energy.

I've heard hundreds of times from the women who come to my events that they've never been listened to like that before. They have simply never been heard with full presence and attention. And on top of that, fully acknowledged and celebrated for what they said.

Women gain confidence when they speak and receive the beam instead of feedback. They find their voices. And when women find their voices, they become fierce women.

Fierce women no longer suffer in silence, because they have claimed their right to speak.

Fierce women speak their truth from their whole being because they have tapped into the power of their bodies.

Fierce women are sovereign, rooted in their self-authority, because they trust the voice within.

Fierce women no longer tolerate anything less than what they deserve because they know their self-worth.

Fierce women stand together in sisterhood because they see their sisters as their allies instead of their enemies.

I believe that fierce women are here to change the world.

I've devoted my life to empowering the leadership of as many women as possible on this planet.

I believe sisterhood, circle, and feminine leadership go hand in hand when we collaborate instead of compete and celebrate each other's greatness instead of putting each other down.

Over the past decade I have taught women all over the world how to lead women's circles. And what I've seen is the biggest challenge women face when stepping into their leadership: owning their voice and becoming more visible in their full power.

I am so committed to this path of uplifting women because this is how we will shift from patriarchy to equality.

I also have two young daughters who I know watch my every move. It is up to me to model what it looks like to be a confident, empowered feminine leader. It is up to me to model conscious, loving sisterhood connection.

The oldest, Kali (talk about fierce! She already lives up to her namesake!), knows what circle is and is mesmerized by my circle videos.

My work is dedicated to teaching other women to model to their daughters this new paradigm of feminine leadership, sisterhood, and circle so that the girls of the next generation are not afraid to use their voices, be bossy, or go after their dreams.

And that's why I am so happy to introduce you to this book. When Rhoda asked me to the write the foreword, I was an immediate yes.

I have an image of her from my event, Feminine Uprising LIVE, which she attended in 2017. The image is riveting. Rhoda is crying while hugging a woman. We had just gone through a deep mother wound process. The vulnerability is palpable.

Fierce women are not ashamed to cry because they know their power is expressed through their raw emotions.

Rhoda has been doing the work to embody her own fierce womanhood, and has brought you into her world with vulnerable, authentic sharing and practices that she already used to bring herself into wholeness. In addition, the practices she shares in this book have done the same for other clients and women in the circles that she's run. I believe they will have the same effect for you.

She begins the book with a story about suffering in silence. This is an epidemic amongst women that must be stopped. Too many women fear that they are either too much (too emotional, too crazy, too intense) or not enough (unworthy, undeserving, and unlovable).

But the opposite is true.

When women understand that they are enough just as they are, that their voice matters, and that they have permission to be themselves, they will start to reclaim their power back and become fiercely committed to what they want and need.

To become a fierce woman, you need to understand this word: EMBODY.

Embodiment describes someone or something that is an example of a quality, an idea, or anything else. This means that you live and breathe it.

It's not something that you know in your head, but in your body.

A fierce woman is an example for other women to see what it looks like to be whole in body, mind, spirit, and heart.

It means you are being a powerful, courageous woman who faces her shadow and accepts all parts of herself.

It means you have done the deeper work so your thoughts, words, and actions are all in alignment.

It means you feel safe enough within yourself to open your heart to give and receive love.

It means you are able to be real, authentic, and vulnerable because you have nothing to hide or be ashamed of.

Rhoda takes you through a process of stepping into this wholeness as a woman and embodying your feminine power. She will teach you the secrets to the questions you're longing to have answered so that you can love yourself more deeply.

Not only that, but her words will feed you like sweet nectar from the goddess herself. She creates a sensory experience with her poetic prose.

She addresses all the secret parts of our womanhood, the things that have become taboo in our culture and deemed as gross or inappropriate, and instead teaches you how to fully love all parts of your lady landscape.

Yes, I'm talking about your breasts, your yoni, and your womb.

It's in loving and recognizing the sheer power of our lady parts that we fully become whole. And from that wholeness, we know who we are.

I hope you enjoy this delicious little book as much I do. And my greatest hope for you is that you give yourself permission to be both soft and fierce, and to rise up into your full glory and power.

Tanya Lynn
Founder, Sistership Circle
August 29, 2018
Author of *Open Your Heart: How to Be a New Generation Feminine Leader*
http://sistershipcircle.com

INTRODUCTION

⸺

THERE WAS THIS GUY I sat down next to on a plane once.

We were flying from San Jose to Los Angeles. A quick fifty-minute flight. I had gone home to visit my parents for the weekend and was traveling back to Southern California, where I lived with my fiancé (now my husband).

Anyhow, this guy on the flight—he kept staring at me for long periods of time. And he was asking all kinds of questions. With each minute that passed, I grew more and more uncomfortable. But the crowded airplane left me with zero options. I couldn't just get up and walk away.

So I sat there. Hoping he'd get the hint, I dished out one- and two-word answers. After fiftteen minutes of this, he seemed to understand. From the corner of my eye, I watched as he pulled a newspaper out of his bag and began to read. Relief rushed through me. I felt a tangle of muscles in my body soften and relax.

Minutes later, over the loudspeaker, the captain was announcing our descent. Another wave of relief. *Soon I would be rid of this guy.* As the plane dipped down from the dark sky, though, the guy started to shift in his seat.

I heard the crinkling of his newspaper, as he whipped it over to his left, toward where I was sitting. And then, very quickly, he positioned the newspaper directly over my lap, so that everything from the bottom of my chest downward was covered. Before I could even begin to comprehend what he was doing, I felt his hand groping my breast. Without even thinking, I dug my elbow into his arm and adjusted my body away from his.

He cleared his throat, closed his newspaper, and sat upright in his seat, pretending that nothing had happened. For the rest of the ride, we sat there, not speaking, not looking at one another. When the plane doors opened, he tore out of there as quickly as he could.

My fiancé was waiting for me at the gate. In those pre-9/11 days, you could do that. He saw my face and knew something was wrong.

"What happened?" he asked.

"This guy on the plane touched my breast," I mumbled.

"What?" my fiancé asked. "Where is he? Which one is he?"

We started to walk toward baggage claim. I saw the back of the guy's head disappear into a cloud of people.

"Please don't. It's okay," I said, not wanting the conflict.

But my fiancé was enraged and wanted to confront the guy. He kept insisting. But I kept pleading for him to let it go. By that time, I couldn't locate the guy anyhow.

I remember, for months after that incident, feeling this deep sense of regret.

I should've used my voice. Why hadn't I?

Shoving him away with my elbow was a hollow gesture. Deep in my womb, I felt like I had missed an opportunity to stand up for myself, to stand up for all women who have ever been groped, assaulted, harassed, or violated in any way.

It made me realize something: I had quieted my voice because I didn't want to make the guy feel uncomfortable. And that realization hit me like a bag of bricks.

Where was my self-worth? And how would I ever locate it amidst a patriarchal environment in which women have been denied the tools and the wisdom to truly know the fullness of what they are?

A couple of years passed before I found the answers I was looking for...

The Thing That Changed Everything

I was twenty-six years old when I started my meditation practice. I didn't know what I was doing exactly, but there was this desire there. This need to dig into the uncharted layers of my life and plunge more deeply into myself.

I remember one of the first meditations that I did. I was in my bedroom, shades drawn, lying back on the bed. Meditating with my attention on the chest, where the heart center is.

And then, just like that... two hours had whizzed by without my realizing it. My body felt suddenly charged by some soothing yet electric kind of energy. I sprung up from the bed. It was as if someone had pressed the "ON" button to my body. I got up to my feet and just stood there. I didn't want to take another step, because I felt so blissfully free—something I had never experienced before—and I was afraid that if I moved any further, the sensation might dissipate.

Then something strange happened. I heard a voice from within. Coming from where exactly, I wasn't sure. But it said the words "You are more powerful than you know."

At first, I'll admit, I was a little freaked out. Then, very slowly, I peered over both of my shoulders as if to say, "Are you talking to me?" Now, I didn't know who was doing the talking. It could've been my own inner self. Could've been a spirit guide, maybe even God. But one thing was clear: that thing the voice was saying, it was palpable. I felt it deep within my being. *That power.* I had never known this kind of feeling before. Such a confident and radiant clarity. There was this deep alignment to my sense of worth, and it was rather striking.

Later on, I realized that my reaction to that voice was severely disempowering. I had initially responded, thinking that I wasn't the one being addressed.

Powerful? Me? I was just Rhoda. That statement surely didn't apply to me.

And that initial thought, that I couldn't be powerful, it broke my heart. Made me realize how much self-love I had been depriving myself of. *For years.*

I know so many women who struggle with this. Who think that they have no right to claim their inherent power. Who quiet their voices and shrink their expression down to bite-sized, manageable bits so as not to create waves, or cause a stir. We hang back in the shadows, waiting for our moment. Hungering for some future time when we're polished enough, smart enough, capable enough, or strong enough.

But let me tell you something: If you keep waiting for the right moment, it will never come. It will elude and evade you. It will turn all of your wild and sacred dreams into dust. Then the power of what you are will not be given the form to express itself. The potential that you possess will be unknown to this world.

I thought back to that time when I had felt powerless on that airplane, too ashamed to stand up for myself—and even too ashamed to have my fiancé stand up for me. I couldn't let something like that happen again. *I wouldn't.* Then and there, the wisdom of *that voice* still resonating in my body, I vowed never to lose my knowing of myself as powerful.

That's why I wrote this book. Women everywhere need to wake up to the power that they possess within. Many of us are already doing so, in a number of different ways.

I look at the television and out on the streets and I see strong women. Strong women standing up and taking ownership of their voices, their bodies, and their truth. It's an exciting time to be a woman in the world. We are clarifying our power and finding the ground beneath our feet—our feet that have walked so far, down so many treacherous and twisting paths, just to fully occupy the space that we are in.

Many cracks are being formed in the culture of the patriarchy. And each and every woman reading these words has contributed to those cracks, to the taking down of a system that has shielded away so much light and potential. If you want to go deeper with me, if you want to fully unlock the power of what you are, keep reading. There is so much to explore and experience. The more a woman knows her power, the more she is able to uplift the world.

Empowered Woman = Empowered Planet

As a woman, you are a universe unto yourself. Vast, mystical, ever unfolding. A vibration of ferocious love and fierce insight. You are a walking revelation. A goddess in all forms: physical, mental, emotional, and spiritual. Your every cell is encoded with vibration, linking everything that you are to the power of the cosmos. Aligning you to the truth that beats at the core of all things.

Reminding you that feminine power is your birthright.

If you're uncertain of what that is exactly, or maybe you've just forgotten: Feminine power is an innate energy that you carry within, one that offers you a direct connection to endless wisdom, strength, and love. It is the unfiltered truth of what you are. It is the fire that burns away all falsehoods, connecting you to the infinite, infusing you with the courage to do, be, and create as you desire, without all of the confines and constructs clouding your essence.

All feminine power, at its essence, is known as Shakti. Many ancient yogic texts point to the power of Shakti as the motor that drives all of life into its deepest expression. Shakti is the energy that is inherent in all things. It's electricity that imbues the entire universe—and every living being within it—with vibration.

You see it at work all around you. Shakti is the force of a waterfall cascading downward. It's that palpable sense of aliveness you feel when you step into the middle of a forest. It's the vibrancy of electric green that radiates from a field of wildflowers.

Shakti is also what animates the breath, the heart, and the dance at play within the cells. In its most powerful form, Shakti is present and known as Kundalini energy, which exists at the base of the spine; when awoken, it can lead to deep spiritual evolution.

This power—this wild feminine force—is naturally within you. In fact, Shakti actually can be felt within the body, once it's understood and channeled properly. It isn't something that needs to be created or developed. There's no need to train exhaustively to reach some kind of exhilarating height. You don't have to meditate for a thousand hours, give away all of your possessions, or find a life coach to "fix" you.

Because the thing is…you don't need fixing. You don't need training or years of development to know this power. It's already there. It's inside, waiting for you to claim it.

It always has been.

You know this.

You've had those moments of conscious knowing, those tingles, those deep body chills that told you there was something more. You've felt the wisdom of that insight in your womb. Those moments in nature, or surrounded by the ones you love.

You know what I mean.

That buzz at the end of a yoga class, when the total peace overtakes you. That state of mad surrender into the arms of a lover who gets you. You've had those experiences that have reached all the way in and touched your soul.

But you thought all of that was meant to be experienced in doses. Here and there. A collection of fleeting moments, flooding in at just the right times to give you that extra boost, or that reminder that all is right in your universe. That's the way most of us live day to day. We let those moments of peace and power be almost accidental. We let them happen to *us*, when instead *we* should be happening to *them*.

To do this, we've got to get deep down in there.

I'm talking deep down, so that you can unearth all of the feminine power that has been buried throughout your inner landscape. That power is alive and ever present, even during those times when you feel like your entire world's shattering around you. Your power is embedded in the precious layers and atoms of your being. It is the foundation of who you are, and no one can pluck it out from under you.

Where you exist, so does your power. Your power is waiting there, amidst all of the cutting thoughts, the ones that play like a broken record. It is waiting there, buried near your spine and in your pelvis, tucked away to nurse old hurts that you've been trying to forget. It is there, sparkling and radiant, underneath the disempowering constructs and beliefs that you've taken on as your own. And once you claim that power, fully and completely, the world will be profoundly impacted by your magical presence, by your ability to just breathe and exist as the awe-inspiring woman that you are. And that power will support you in whatever it is you choose to undertake and express, whether it's speaking your truth, launching your business, becoming a mother, ending world hunger, shattering a trillion glass ceilings, or all of the above.

That time I meditated and heard that voice was such a monumental moment for me. The possibility of who I was expanded, then and there. All because I cleared away the chatter and the fear from my mind, so that I could listen more deeply to the truth within me.

You can learn to listen more deeply to discover your truth too. And not just listen, but *feel* and *experience*. *Fierce Woman* will show you how to do that. It's a text of illumination, of expanding into the possibilities by way of action, movement, breath, connection, love, and surrender. My background is heavily rooted in the practice of tantra, which is a way of understanding and experiencing the world through unity. Seeing and knowing all aspects as one, so that light and dark, black and white, sun and moon are no longer separate, but integrated in deep harmony. This love-based understanding has colored all the many pages that you have in your hands right now.

In this book, I've created a way for you to come back to who you truly are, full force—a woman awake and pulsing with wild knowing. The book is broken down into four sections: mind, body, heart, and spirit. Each section symbolizes a reclaiming of yet more feminine power to be uncovered within you.

There's no wrong way to experience this book. These pages offer up a massive serving of truth, and you've got to integrate all of it in your own way. Almost every chapter contains an exercise, or something actionable that you can do to bless your beautiful life. So do a chapter and an exercise a day, if that speaks to you. Or power through several chapters and exercises, if you're feeling the momentum. Trust in your own inner wisdom, and you will get the exact experience you need from this book.

And let me just say: I wrote this straight from the heart. Sitting in cafés and lying on my stomach in my indoor teepee. All charged up on love, green tea, and Shakti. So there is an energy that is coursing through every sentence, one that I hope you will feel in your body and heart. So that your truth, your authentic power as a woman, will rise and be expressed on this planet. No longer a secret, no longer relegated to the corner shadows. No longer quieted or shut down or made to feel ashamed.

You decided to come here. To this time and place. To this body. You yearned for this experience from afar. And now you are here, living it. You are here, in the power of your magnificent form.

This is for you. These words, these intentions, this love—all of this was created for you, goddess sister. To remind you that you are a powerful woman, worthy of every last dream that you've had the courage to carry in your heart.

This is deep stuff. Gigantic stuff.

So let's take a breath and begin.

SECTION 1
⇒ MIND ⇐

WHAT YOU THINK ABOUT BECOMES YOU

—————

When I was in my early twenties, I was living in Los Angeles, trying to make it as an actress. It was a tough time. Weeks would pass without a single audition. I cycled through an assortment of off-colored jobs, just to keep myself afloat. Some of the highlights of my odd Hollywood jobs included being a waitress at a strip club, a blackjack player at a local casino (hired and trained by the casino to outsmart the other players and keep the money in the "house"), a massage therapist, a receptionist at a post-production facility, background talent, a model for local advertisements, and a performer who toured high schools and spoke to kids about HIV prevention.

I often felt as if I was going in a million different directions…and getting absolutely nowhere.

Here's the thing, though: There was one constant on my mind. Amidst all of the chaos of my daily life, I kept this one vision going all the time. It was a fantasy, really. Almost like a constant refrain. I would often catch myself daydreaming…and in these daydreams, I was this sexy siren of a jazz singer, belting out old standards on a stage in a smoky bar somewhere.

I know what you're thinking. How ridiculously random.

And I get where you're coming from. But see, ever since I had discovered the music of Ella Fitzgerald, I carried that vision. At the age of sixteen, I had come upon one of her CDs in a local record store—a collection of Gershwin songs. I took it home and ended up playing it all day and night. Her voice transported me. I had never heard anything like it, and I was absolutely mystified.

I started carving out these fantasies in my mind. Seeing myself as a jazz singer. My hair a certain way. Dressed in a gown. Awe-inspired faces gazing up at me.

And one day—out of absolutely nowhere—the fantasies came true.

I auditioned for a film that just so happened to be looking for a jazz vocalist. Within days of my first audition, I was offered the role.

Flash forward to weeks later. I was in the trailer, getting made up. It was everything I had seen in my fantasies. Same hair. Same dress. Same smoky bar. Same audience looking up at me. It was as if someone had dipped into my head and read every single detail.

That was when I got it. *What you think about becomes you.*

I hadn't taken a single effort to make this jazz vocalist dream come true, and yet there it was.

My mind had brought it to me effortlessly—every detail of it—without my taking a single action toward making it happen. I had been working toward the actress thing for many months, but had never thought to seek out opportunities to sing jazz. But that didn't matter. *It still happened.*

How is this possible? And how can you utilize this wisdom to create the kind of life you want?

It all has to do with energy and vibration. And guess what? Whether you know it or not, you've been involved in this dance with energy and vibration for your whole life, calling to you whatever it is that you're thinking about.

Here's a quick primer on energy to get you understanding it a little more.

Everything Is Energy

Everything that you are is made up of energy.

You are a maze of vibration and undulation. A spine-tingling composition, overflowing with waves and pulses. Inner and outer resonance, blending into all things. Expressing and articulating what lies at the core of you. That undefinable something. That something that is everything.

You know what I mean, don't you? You feel it there, sometimes. When you've got clarity. Or when you've just made love. Or when joy somersaults across your chest, as you see something you're creating come to life. There's this energy. This frequency that raises the hairs on the back of your neck, making you feel as if you are one with everything.

In these moments, you are seeing through the veil. Beyond the thick, heavy wrinkles of its fabric. You are feeling yourself as a part of something greater.

And that is because you *are* a part of something greater.

The truth is that we are all energetic beings, living in a world that is entirely made up of energy. Beneath the surface of all things, that energy is throbbing with deep intention.

Depending upon the quality of your thoughts, your energy will hold a certain kind of vibration. There are varying degrees of vibration at play in this material world at all times. Some vibrations operate in lower realms; these kinds of vibrations are felt as dense, heavy, rigid, consumed in fear. Think about what happens in your body when you watch a movie that's crammed full of depravity and violence. The vibration in you goes dim, gets weighed down. But when you're watching something that inspires and awakens you, your vibration automatically rises. You feel lighter, expansive, grateful for the air you breathe. This is a higher vibration. And a higher vibration is more magnetic than a lower one. It can attract, create, and manifest at a much more rapid pace.

Each one of us vibrates in our own unique way. And the thought is the starting point, the blueprint that creates the world you wake up to each day. Every single thing that you think and dream, every inkling and inclination that you invite in to fill the chambers of your mind, makes an impact. It turns a new page, or drives the old groove in deeper.

Whether you're conscious of it or not, you determine how you show up. And you've been doing this for years.

Look around you. Look at the things that fill up your life right now. The only thing all of those elements have in common is you. You are the center of your universe. And the things you consciously think shape and inform every particle of your inner and outer existence.

Thoughts = Vibration

Thoughts are like limbs, always reaching and extending outward, pulling toward you the things that you are focused upon.

Never underestimate a thought, and all the power that it contains within it. It is like a tightly-packed kernel, ready to burst into the realm of potential. Ready to make either a hell or a heaven out of your life, depending upon what you're thinking.

Each thought that gets etched into the surface of your mind creates a result. If you think to yourself that you're not worthy, that will be your reality; those thoughts will extend beyond the mind, rippling throughout your entire being. They will shape the way you move and speak. They will hunch your shoulders over as you walk, they will stifle your magic, they will temper your expression. People and circumstances will materialize in ways that prove you right and show you just how unworthy you are.

What you think determines your vibration.

Never forget this.

Carry this wisdom in your womb as if your existence depends upon it.

In many ways, it does.

Because if you spend your every day entertaining thoughts that cut down the beauty of what you are, your life will reflect that right back to you. And so you must brush aside all disempowering thought so that the truth of your power can come forward.

I know how hard that sounds, especially in a world where women's minds have been co-opted, and we've been led to believe that what we are is no match for what men are.

Our minds are so used to taking in all the impoverished messaging about the potential of women. The way we are objectified in advertisements, magazines, TV shows, films, and commercials—we might not realize it as it's happening, but all of it is shaping the way we see ourselves and our value. The cultural perception of what women are—of what we represent—is some toned-down, muted version of the true reality. Our minds have become so accustomed to thinking about ourselves and our bodies as less than what they are. And if we let the mind stay comfortable in this limited perception, then we will never know the enormous power that we possess. We will never know ourselves as strong, worthy, capable women, which is what we truly are.

So you've got to tap into the mental realm. Get down in there. Engage your thoughts. Don't let random dribbles of low vibration play out in your mind. Realize that you're driving the car and it is up to you, at all times, which way to turn.

Your thoughts each have their own pitch. Each pitch cuts through time and space, making connections with all other pitches in existence. This is exactly why you're able to magnetize your own life circumstances. It starts with the thought. Allow your mind to focus on the reasons why you don't deserve love, and your vibration will be like one of those foam memory pillows; it will change the shape of its contours to support you.

Wake Up, Badass Woman

When you start aligning the potency of your thoughts to words, feeling, and energies that vibrate higher, you wake up. You start to move like someone who knows her power. You become a woman whose definition extends beyond the set confines of a fear-based culture. You actually carve out your own definition. In your own dictionary. No one else can lay claim to this. No one else can alter it, no matter how hard they try.

Your mind is like a kind of mystical plane. Endless. Sparkling with possibilities. This space is waiting for you to infuse it. It's waiting for you to determine, to remember, who you truly are.

You contain within your body a network of unlimited potential. That potential, that energy, does not merely swirl and move within you. It extends beyond your physical body, animating everything in its presence. You walk into a room with a high kind of vibration, and the difference is palpable. The people in the room might not be entirely aware of it, but somewhere inside of them, they will feel the change. They will notice their own energy come up. They will sense a kind of ease that has seeped out into the space.

Vibration is undeniable. It determines and informs everything we see around us. So why not use it to re-create our lives? To fully feel ourselves as powerful women, thundering with vibrancy, creativity, and love?

This might sound daunting to you. It might sound a little out there to actually think that you can change your universe by transforming your thoughts, thereby transforming the vibration that you are.

But it's possible. Whether you want to sing jazz or travel to all 195 countries of the world.

You can make this happen, regardless of what you've experienced in your life.

Every woman reading this book comes here with her own stories. Her own fears, desires, passions, and projections.

To begin this journey of amplifying your natural vibration, you must first feel into it. Feeling the natural vibration of who you are will create the kind of environment that will contribute to the rise of empowering thoughts. And then those empowering thoughts, in turn, will boost your vibration, and on and on…

Take a moment to do these exercises.

⇢ *power exercise for* ⇠
RAISING YOUR VIBRATION, PART I

Preparing for the Exercise

If you can, find a quiet spot where you won't be disturbed. You can take any position that's comfortable for you. You can sit, lie down, get in a fetal position—whatever you feel your body needs at the moment.

Doing the Exercise

Let your jaw drop open and breathe into your body.

Close your eyes and scan your insides for any hint of vibration.

Once you've found that vibration in your body, just stay locked on it. Breathe into it and bring your focus to it. Pour all attention there.

As you do so, don't be surprised if you feel deep joy. This is your natural state, and reconnecting to its potency might be alarming.

As you feel into your own unique vibration, say these words, either out loud or in your head:

My natural vibration is one of love and expansion.

Repeat this a few times before ending the meditation.

And if you're unable to locate the vibration, just breathe deeply into your body and say the words to yourself. This will spark something in your unconscious and help you to connect with that inner vibration. Don't struggle with this and think you're not doing it right if you initially can't feel anything. The majority of us weren't given the tools and encouragement to make space for aligning to our own unique vibration, to the power of our energy. So this might take some practice and time for you. But don't let that bring discouragement. Just set the intention to align to your vibration, and allow whatever is there to come up.

You can keep the vibrancy of your thoughts clear and high by settling into your own vibration, again and again.

The feeling will help to shape the thoughts. If you stay anchored in your natural vibration all day, it will be more difficult for the thoughts to rebel and dip into the pool of low frequency.

Another way to harness your vibration is through the next exercise. It will help you to release your attachment to old fear-based thoughts, so that you can start to welcome in new ones.

⇥ *power exercise for* ⇤
RAISING YOUR VIBRATION, PART 2

Preparing for the Exercise

You'll need a pen and a journal (or some blank paper) for this one.

Doing the Exercise

Think about your own stories and the ways that you've let them limit the natural essence of what you are. Start to write about these stories. Write about how your truest, most authentic self has been stifled by those stories, by the past that should be behind you. Write for as long as you need to.

Now, think about the ways in which these stories have actually empowered you. It might be challenging, but you can do it. Find the gold amidst all the murk.

What lesson did these particular stories teach you? Did they make you stronger, more aware? Did they call for you to make some kind of big change in your life? Every dip into the valley, every low in life, carries with it some kind of teaching. Write positively about the ways in which you've gathered some form of new understanding, perspective, strength, or healing from the difficult stories in your life.

As you write about the positive, feel the way the energy in your body soars. Stay rooted and connected in this feeling. Write about your commitment to stay anchored in your natural vibration.

Extra Badass Tip

After the exercise, close your eyes. Take the vibration of the feeling that has been created into your heart and breathe it in for one minute. Stay tapped into this place as you open your eyes.

⇒ power exercise for ⇐
TAKING CONTROL OF YOUR THOUGHTS

Preparing for the Exercise

This is one that should be interwoven into your whole day. Before you start, take a few breaths to become present in your body.

Doing the Exercise

This is something that I know will work wonders for you: spend the entire day staying in the center of each and every thought.

What that means is that you're not just letting your thoughts run like background music in an elevator. Be completely and totally tuned in. Sit in the center of everything that gets processed in your mind. This means that you're not trying to do a million things while the thought is happening. It means that as the thought is forming, you stop and listen to it. Feel that you are sitting directly at its core, tapped into it. Imagine that your entire being pools into the very middle of this thought.

Doing this accomplishes something very important. It puts you right at the heart of the thought. It makes you completely aware and locked in to it. This is a position of deep intention, where you can control what moves in and out. Don't let thoughts overtake and engulf you in the usual ways. Sit in the center of each one. That's your power position.

When I'm in the middle of a thought, it often feels very soothing. But if I'm not being fully present with each thought, guess what happens? My mind becomes assaulted with an endless flood of thoughts. And let me just say that they're generally not of an empowering nature.

Usually, we let our thoughts dictate the script, and it's as if we're just following the lead as puppets in their control. But when you arrive at the center of the thought, you're no longer playing its game. You're breathing into it and situating yourself inside of it with so much awareness that you take the power back. You're in control. You start realizing that by sitting in the center of a thought, you can call the shots.

Once you are there so totally with every thought, you can then interrupt a negative thought before it pulverizes you. Or you can grow a positive thought into a big, beautiful wildflower that will amplify your essence. Stopping and sitting in the center of a positive thought makes the energy of that thought more powerful. And it makes the possibility of more positive thoughts to follow even higher.

So. Do. It.

Try this today. You will feel the gorgeous sparks of your mind flowing outward, inviting you to experience yourself at a deeper and more vibrant level.

BOOM.

THINK YOU'RE NOT GOOD ENOUGH? HERE'S WHY YOU'RE WRONG

———

IN HIGH SCHOOL I had a desire so deep that it nearly burned a hole in me.

My fantasy was to one day be a part of the girls' basketball team.

The problem was, despite the gravity of this desire, the fear of putting myself out there was severe. Every time mention of try-outs came up, I looked the other way and pretended that it didn't mean anything to me. I didn't even tell my friends about it. Just kept it locked away inside myself.

But all of that changed when I hit my third year of high school. Something propelled me to go for it. Maybe it was the confidence of gaining upperclassman status; I'm not quite sure. Whatever it was, I felt compelled enough to move on it, despite the fear that was still present inside of me.

During the tryout period, I pushed myself immensely. Running laps, doing sit-ups, shooting basket after basket. I had always been athletic, and loved every moment of gym class, but had never tried out for an actual team before. Many of the girls there had been a part of the team from years prior.

I remember watching them during tryouts. The ease. The confidence. The clarity. Even though I was holding my own on the court, I'd often see another girl do something impressive and instantly start doubting my own worth. I started questioning myself. What was I even doing there? What special thing could I possibly bring to the team when all of these girls had such obvious gifts on display?

To my surprise, I ended up making it through the first cut. There was a moment of sheer elation. They wanted me, at least for now. *They thought I was good enough.*

But the elation soon shifted back into fear. With only the strongest, most skillful girls left after the cut, I felt like it would be even more glaringly obvious that I was the weak one in the bunch.

And so I did something that is kind of embarrassing to admit...

I never came back to tryouts.

I had actually survived the first cut, but I was too afraid to continue. Too afraid of them eventually uncovering my weaknesses and rejecting me. So I did what I thought was the sane thing—I rejected them first. And I never, ever tried out for any other sports team again.

You see what happened there?

Even when an outside source confirmed to me that I was good enough, I still wasn't convinced of my worth. The fear was just too crippling. It told me to go home, to stop being led by some silly desire.

Not knowing how to rebel against that voice, I listened to it. I convinced myself that I knew something that those basketball coaches didn't. Where they saw a girl who was worthy of making the cut, I saw a girl who would never measure up. Those were two very different realities, both of which were correct.

Whatever you believe in your mind is what is real and true.

If you cultivate thoughts that cut you down, that threaten your sense of self-worth, then your every moment will be created from those thoughts.

When a woman makes the choice to shift her thoughts, her world shifts as a result. The booming voice of fear starts to break apart; it gets choppier and more difficult to decipher.

Back in high school, I didn't realize that there was another reality out there, one in which I could shine and live in alignment with my true power. Going home and never coming back seemed like the most logical reaction to me. Looking back on it now, I cringe at the opportunity that I missed.

Three Words That Every Woman Must Learn to Unlearn

Not good enough.

The weight of those three words sits heavy in so many women.

How many times have the words "not good enough" held a woman or girl back? How many female athletes, business owners, film directors, inventors, doctors, tech magnates, and presidents have we missed out on simply because of the words "not good enough"?

But also:

What about those times when a woman blazes on despite those words, "not good enough"? This is a woman who has convinced herself otherwise. Who is in firm alignment with her worth and has her eye trained on the prize ahead. As focused and strong as she is, she will most likely bump up against resistance in the process. The mantra of "not good enough" will make attempts to flood her awareness through other voices, forces, and faces around her. There will be an effort to deter her from getting where she wants to go. Others will look on, stone-faced and full of bitterness; they will grab her by the arm and try to remind her that she is lacking.

This is because whenever a woman builds up the courage to stand in her power, facing off against all of the tired beliefs and unsustainable systems in the process, other people get uncomfortable. This puts massive pressure on women, as we have a penchant for setting others at ease, not intimidating anyone or making them feel less than.

But that's an old story. Rising up requires forging a new path. If we want to do away with the incessant fear-based thoughts that are premised on our not being good enough, we must actively work toward emboldening the mind.

The mental energies of a woman are imbued with the force of lightning.

Your body is coursing with electricity. There is a quiet buzz, deep within, that is seeking liberation. Your thoughts are what light the match. Knowing that you are good enough, that you are not lacking, is the beginning. It's the start of that grand quest to reclaim all the parts of you that have gotten lost over time.

→ power exercise for ←
KNOWING YOU ARE GOOD ENOUGH

Preparing for the Exercise

Immerse yourself in this exercise every day and you will shine like the stunning, radiant, badass woman that you truly are.

Doing the Exercise

In the morning, right after you rise, press your hands against your heart. Say to yourself: *I am worthy.* Feel that worth percolating in your cells. Like love. *Because you are good enough.*

During the day, admire every storm cloud. Find iridescence swirling in a stranger's eyes. Let the sounds of leaves crushing under your feet overtake you. In all of it, see—*feel*—the inherent beauty that trembles beneath the surface. Know that beauty as your own. Because *you are good enough.*

When the sunlight hits your face and you feel its luxurious rays penetrating your every pore, melt. Know in your body that you have a right to be here, to occupy the space that you are in at this very moment. Let that conviction intermingle with your blood and with all of the tears you've ever shed. *Because you are good enough.*

At night, before you go to sleep, get on your knees and press your forehead to the ground. Imagine your mind emptying all the things that have kept you stagnant. Imagine you are pouring those things into the earth.

Whisper "farewell" and feel your mental landscape expanding into infinity.

You are good enough.

If you can always remember that, then you have my blessing to forget everything else.

QUIETING THE JUDGMENTAL
VOICE WITHIN

SOME YEARS BACK, MY husband and I decided that we would both go a week without making a single judgment.

It was the hardest week of our lives. But also seriously worth it. We ended up realizing just how often the mind defaults to judgment, criticism, and negativity. Not just toward ourselves, but toward the people and circumstances around us. Once we started interrupting this pattern, we felt as if a tractor had been lifted off of our backs. Things just flowed more smoothly. We were more connected, open, available.

Cause the thing is, judgments and criticism? Those things are the opposite of love. We drain the best parts of ourselves whenever we make judgments. A judgment is like a net. It captures your lowest inclinations. Extinguishes the essence. Strangles the natural beauty of what is. Restricts love and amplifies fear.

When you judge yourself, or others, your aura becomes a thick cloud. Your eyes lose their glow. The muscles constrict.

31

Stress gets kicked up in the nervous system. Your emotions start to tie themselves up in knots. Feelings of depression, anxiety, loneliness, and melancholy might even start to creep in.

Whenever you have a judgmental thought, your energy naturally dips. The beautiful parts of you retreat; you withdraw and withhold in ways that are unnatural to your spirit.

The need to criticize or judge is based in fear. Instead of giving ourselves over to the moment and accepting everyone and ourselves as amazing beings worthy of love, we take a step back. We separate ourselves from what is, instead of opening our arms to it.

The brush that the mind paints with creates the portrait of our reality. So if you're painting with a brush dipped in fear and criticism, your environment will reflect that. You will constantly be presented with things and people that are going to push your buttons and drive yet more judgment from you. The cycle will continue unless you take a stand and interrupt it.

Are You Willing To?

Because now's the time. For women, especially. We are powerful and magnetic beings, and when we start to make judgments about the women around us, we're not only bringing down their vibration, but we're bringing down our own vibration as well.

Your body and mind will read your judgment as something you feel about your own self. And so the vibration of your judgments, no matter who you're judging, will stick to your own frequency. A negative thought, word, or action—regardless of whether it's toward another person or yourself—will short out your own vibration.

If you notice yourself criticizing or judging someone, stop and become aware of what you're really doing. Oftentimes what we see is reflecting an aspect of ourselves right back to us. If we can start becoming aware of how our judgments are connected to the way we feel about ourselves, that's like being given a gift; it's presenting us with a major opportunity to evolve and completely transform our lives.

Another thing to keep in mind: If you judge another woman, it doesn't matter that you're holding your tongue and keeping the thought from her. The fact that you're merely thinking of it is powerful enough to tamper with the energy that she exudes. Thoughts are mightier and more impactful than we give them credit for. When you harbor judgments about other people, you're shorting out their light.

You know the saying, "If you don't have something nice to say, don't say it at all"?

That never really sat right with me. It doesn't go deep enough.

Can you imagine a person who walks around all day with negative fragments swirling in their head, not finding any kind of expression for them? That's a nervous breakdown waiting to happen.

The key, instead, is to bring yourself to a place where you are simply being and operating from a vibration of love, so that those judgmental, fear-based thoughts aren't dominating the inner conversation. It's about deciding to step into your power, so that you can create the life that you want. See the criticisms and the judgments as the dead weight that they are, so that you can overcome them.

Don't Let Your Desire for Safety Stop
You from Living Full-Out

Now, am I saying to spend the rest of your life walking around like a doe-eyed fawn who trusts everything and everyone?

Not at all.

You still have to protect yourself in life. You shouldn't go searching for strangers to embrace in dark alleyways, just to show the world what a nonjudgmental and loving woman you are. By all means, keep yourself safe, sister. Exercise your right to use discernment to stay secure and protected.

But be careful of the places in life where you've let your attachment to safety put you out of alignment with the real, authentic you. Watch for the ways in which you automatically shift into the gear of separation, driving gaps between you and the ones who should be close to you.

Sometimes, these thoughts might feel uncontrollable. They might seduce you into believing that you have no choice. That you're stuck with the state of mind that you currently have. But you're not.

You're a goddess who has every right to be in the driver's seat of this divine adventure.

This divine adventure that is your life is also your art.

You must make this art consciously and with unwavering presence. You must let your every cell be consumed by it.

A Present Mind Is Essential

When you're present, there's no space for judgment. The energy of judgment and criticism cannot flourish in a mind that is in the here and now. A present mind is tapped into the flow of reality. Being present means that you're open and accepting.

A busy mind has great difficulty accepting what is and embracing each change as it comes. It's too caught up in the noise within. It's too charged with trying to prove itself.

There's also a need for the mind to make things logical, to shut everything away in the proper boxes so that it all makes sense. Too much energy comes with pursuing these pointless goals, and then there is nothing leftover to use in service of love.

Think about what it's like when you have a delicious thought—one that is surging with the qualities of joy, positivity, peace, and acceptance. These are the thoughts that make the whole body come to life. They raise your vibration and electrify your sense of being and purpose.

This is the opposite of what happens when we're judging someone else. When we're looking at a woman and wondering why she has the nerve to wear a particular outfit when she needs to lose twenty more pounds. Or when we become fixated on someone else's hair color, or the sound of their high-pitched laugh. Or when we criticize ourselves for not being good enough, for not being fun enough or lovable enough or drop-dead gorgeous enough.

⇥ power exercise for ⇤
RELINQUISHING THE JUDGMENTAL VOICE WITHIN
Preparing for the Exercise

Start out by making a commitment to relinquish all judgments for one single day. (This might seem impossible, but it's worth a shot, right?) I like to do this at least the night before, and not the morning of. If you make the commitment the night before and allow yourself to "sleep on it," the energy of this commitment will settle into your unconscious and help to strengthen your resolve for the next day.

Doing the Exercise

When you wake up to start your day, stay in bed for a moment and visualize. See yourself standing at the edge of a turquoise ocean. Feel the sun on your face. Imagine a great wave approaching. But instead of fearing it, surrender to it. See yourself opening your arms, as if you are preparing to embrace the charging wave. As the wave comes, let it completely overtake you. Imagine it cleansing you of all your judgments. Feel your inner critic being swept away into the endless water.

Revel in the clarity of your mind and your heart. By relieving yourself of the need to judge, you can now show up as the powerhouse of a woman that you naturally are.

And then, the important part: get out of bed and go a whole day without judging.

It's going to test you like crazy at first. You might be tempted to give up a couple dozen times. But keep at it.

If you drift into a judgmental thought, catch yourself. Breathe, focus on your heart, and let go of the thought.

You have my word that by letting the thought go, you are not losing a single thing. Instead, you're gaining the keys to the paradise that is the clear and vibrant mind.

YOU ARE SIMPLY TOO FIERCE FOR THE STATUS QUO

I REMEMBER THIS STORY my dad once told me.

The year was 1963. My dad was working in Silicon Valley as a training manager for the company Philco.

One day, he found himself in a conversation with the personnel manager. They were discussing parts of Betty Friedan's book *The Feminine Mystique*, which had just come out. (My dad was always a strong supporter of women and all things feminine power, and it makes me smile thinking that he read that book upon its release!)

During their discussion, they started to think about their own work environment. They realized that out of their three hundred-person division, 75 percent of the employees were women. But not a single one of those women held a management position of any kind.

This finding struck my dad and the personnel manager as deeply abysmal. Together, they teamed up and decided that they would offer management training classes that were specifically for women, in the hopes that they would eventually start moving up the ranks and into higher positions.

After spreading the word about these classes, my dad was surprised to discover that not a single woman in their division was interested. To add to that, all of their male supervisors shrugged the idea off as a complete waste of time.

It's obvious that the women from my dad's old company were holding on to beliefs that told them that they weren't management material. And so they stayed small, opting for the safe embrace of the status quo.

But let me tell you something about the status quo: It never holds up. It's just an illusion that exists to coddle the conscious mind, which craves the idea of safety, no matter the cost.

Have you ever felt your heart quicken at the thought of taking a risk, but then your mind swooped in and stopped you? Has your body ever gotten warm at the idea of you breaking out of your shell to experience the fullness of your life...but then the conscious mind stepped in like the droopy naysayer that it is, reminding you that this new reality would rip away any semblance of security?

In its quest for never-ending safety, the conscious mind has walled too many of us women off from our power. From saying or doing the things that make our hearts come alive. Instead, we withhold. We continue to worship the flimsy state of status quo, which is a complete fabrication of reality, since it doesn't exist.

You Just Changed a Little Bit While You Read This Sentence (How Amazing Is That?!)

Think about it: every year, every day, every second, the form of what you are is changing.

The energy of the body—the blood, the cells, the lymph—is shifting through various formations. With every breath you take, you are drinking in new oxygen, and the new frequency of this is entering your being. The changing forms of the environment that surround you have an impact on you as well.

The colors, the smells, and the textures of each season, of each day, of each new piece of information you receive, bring something different to your vibration.

This is something that cannot be stopped.

The feminine body is the radiant expression of this one simple truth: You are a cyclical being. In you, right now, you hold the keys to birth and death. The energies of creation and destruction are flowing through your body, in equal force. You were made to flow, to move freely through the cycles, the waxing and waning of the moon, the softening and hardening of nature.

To rally against this would be to deny what is.

You were not meant for the status quo.

You were meant for so much more.

If you are trying to hold on to ideas of safety and security, if you don't have the courage to step out onto the ledge and embrace what you know, deep in your heart, should be the next phase of your journey, then you've got to disentangle yourself from the incessant chatter of the conscious mind. Otherwise, it'll keep you stuck and rooted in your fear.

If You Continue to Think the Same Thoughts, You Will Keep Getting the Same Results

Burn down the altar of the status quo.

Let the smoke rise, let the ashes fall where they may.

Break up the monotony of the comfortable rhythms you're accustomed to.

Otherwise, the spirit in you will become a weak gasp of air, trembling for more expansion.

The women at my dad's old company wanted nothing to do with moving up the ladder because they were used to seeing only men as managers, and to even entertain the thought that they could reach that level threatened their sense of safety.

Now, if you are choosing to stay safe at the expense of your true self, of the dreams and visions that you carry, then you must take a breath and resist.

Resist the urge to keep your light hidden. Resist the sense of security that comes from staying stuck in the known. Resist the parts of you that would like to deny your brilliance, because you're too afraid of expressing the fullness of what you are.

Your vibration is precious. The woman that you are is meant to exist in an ongoing spiral of exploration and expansion. An inner and outer current of vibrancy, expressing itself through every movement, every thought, every breath. There is so much power to tap in the mind that you have.

Here's an exercise you can do to rain on the parade of any old, played-out thoughts that are keeping you in the status quo:

→ *power exercise for* ←
TRIPPING UP YOUR MENTAL STATUS QUO

Preparing for the Exercise

Grab a pen and a journal (or some blank pieces of paper).

Doing the Exercise

Think about a disempowering belief that you carry about yourself. Just one.

Write it down on paper, whatever it is. For example:

> *I'm a disaster at relationships.*
> *I can never be confident.*
> *I'm ashamed of my body.*
> *I've fallen way behind in my life.*
> *Everyone I know is doing better than me.*
> *I'm too weird.*
> *Nobody wants me.*
> *Nobody loves me.*
> *Nobody cares.*

But remember: just pick one.

Freeze your instinct to let it all spill. Settle in and focus on one belief that's holding you back. Stare at the words on the page and breathe them in.

Feel this belief as the thing that's keeping your mental status quo in a satisfied cocoon of disempowerment.

Now, pick up the pen again and write out one action you could take that goes against it. You know what I'm saying?

So if you think that you're a disaster in your relationships, reach out to a loved one and have a genuine conversation. If you think that you don't have confidence, decide to do something that scares you and builds your courage. If you're ashamed of your body, spend the evening lathering your gorgeous naked self in delicious oils, so that you can feel the natural beauty of your physical form.

Take the action that will help you to step away from your mental status quo. And once you take it, feel it. Feel the way your body, mind, and heart respond. Feel the new energy coursing through you and breathe it all the way in.

And even after you do this, try to go about your life with the intention of acting like a woman who will not be shut down by baseless beliefs. You deserve a life of flow, one that takes you beyond the status quo, so that you might tumble forward and collide into the center of your wildest dreams.

YOU CAN CREATE
WHATEVER YOU WANT

———

THE PAINTINGS OF FRIDA Kahlo, the books of Maya Angelou, the billion-dollar empire that Oprah has constructed. All of these creations have just one thing in common: They didn't exist at one time. They had to be created, visioned into form, in order to become emblazoned onto this material plane.

Now, I know this is obvious, but it's worth drawing your attention to. Because as women we tend to doubt our dreams. To render them impossible and stuff them away in a drawer somewhere.

But I'm here to remind you: If there is a dream in your heart, you can make it a reality. You have that ability. That power.

What you want to create for yourself might not exist physically in the world yet. But don't let that discourage you. Don't let it stop you. If Frida Kahlo, Maya Angelou, and Oprah had gotten too discouraged to continue moving toward their dreams, imagine all the beauty and joy that our world would have never known.

If you shut off your inner light (because that's what you'll essentially be doing if you choose not to go for your dreams), the world will miss out on all the wonder that you were born to express within it.

Let the discouragement go. Set down your fears, shed all of the disappointments. Stop working against yourself, stop fighting the natural wisdom you carry within. That natural wisdom wants to be fully expressed in the world, and a huge part of that expression comes from you living out your dreams, full force.

Ready to Go There?

The first step is to be courageous enough to carve out the vision. To even go there. Because so many of us don't. So many of us give up before even taking the time to see, or create in our minds, what is possible.

Every creation starts inside of you.

Fragments of a book, the textures of a painting, the half notes of a song. Ideas for launching a business or inventing something. That call, from deep within, to light the match and start the rebellion that tips the scale.

Whatever it is you'd like to manifest, the energy of creation must dwell within before it can be realized out on the physical plane. Before your creation can be birthed, it must be cultivated and nurtured in the body, mind, and heart.

When a woman becomes pregnant, she first nurtures the baby in her womb, so that it can grow and develop. As her body does this sacred work, she holds the vision of what her new life will look like. She plans. Imagines. Cultivating this dream that is evolving inside of her. Relying upon her heart to feel her way through this exciting process. The magic that is happening within her stirs and stirs, until it is ready to be birthed.

Whatever it is you would like to create, that magic is there, waiting for you to stir it. And by stir it, I mean *lock into the vision of what you desire.* If you can see it, it can be yours. If you can't see it, if you can't do the work of imagining, without limits, what you can do and create, then it will be difficult to procure it.

Without a vision, without something to lock into, the electricity of creation will fizzle out. The landscape of your mind will lack the clarity to create or to drive you into meaningful action.

To lock into the vision of what you desire means to imagine exactly what that vision looks like once it's made into a reality. The first thing you must do is to see beyond the lack so that you can welcome in the possibility. The potential.

If you get stuck on all the reasons why what you want to create will not work, this will kill the vibe. You'll lower your frequency. The energies of creation cannot bloom upon feelings of lack and fear, or on excuses. Creation needs fertile ground to work with. Your mind becomes fertile ground when it's focused on holding the vision of that thing you are determined to create.

Let's say you want to write a book. You've got to see the finished product. The cover design, the layout, the crisp, white pages. The size of the book, the way the font looks. All of the thousands of words filling up the pages. That's the vision.

If you're tempted to start visualizing yourself at book signings or speaking engagements, you can do that, once in a while. But I encourage you to stay focused on the finished product, on what you have the power to create. This will refine and sharpen your ability to make it tangible. You've got to make sure not to lose your vision of what the finished product will look like. This will help you honor the high-vibrating creative powers that you possess within. This will wake up something deep inside of you. It will tangle you up in that feeling of anything being possible. And that feeling—*right in the middle* of that precious feeling—is where you want to be.

The Future Is Pregnant with Possibilities

If anything is possible, if you truly believe that, then you can take empty space and actually fill it with something. You can take your hands, which are full of so much potential, and you can mold something from nothing.

You can do it. You were born to create. In order for you yourself to be created in this world, creative energies had to be used by the Source, the Creator, or God (take your pick).

Can you imagine?

Stop and breathe that in for a moment.

What power there must be inside of you.

You were created from the greatest source of love and light that there is, and that doesn't just dissipate when you're born. That creativity is still there, swirling within your beautiful being. You are lit up by it. One with it. This is why there is a yearning, a pull, toward creating, always. This is why you are always looking at the pieces and imagining what can be. It's why you are always looking for ways to express yourself, to shape and beautify, to bring new color and life to the world around you.

→ affirmation for ←
CREATIVITY

Creativity comes so naturally to me
I breathe it in and out,
Effortlessly.
I sway to the rhythm of the cycles that hold me
I bow to the line of women that came before me
I feel their heartbeats synchronized with my own
I feel my body, as a river
Of Creativity and Manifestation
I feel the Source of all Creativity
Deep within me
Nudging me toward expression
Toward expansion
I have the ability to create all I desire.
The possibilities are endless.

It's No Accident That We Know Nature as "Mother"

When you're out in nature, when you get so lost in it that you feel yourself merging into it, *that* is the power of creation and the feminine's role in that creation. The contours of your feminine body hold endless mysteries and codes. The womb, the spine, the heart. The energies of creation are ever present and available in the receptive and flowing body of woman.

She gives life, she nurtures, she nourishes, she grows, she roots downward and transforms upward. She is an all-powerful force. A fierce alchemy of love and acceptance. Shattering what is safe to create what is sacred.

The vision is what sets all this in motion. Cultivate the vision of what you want to create, and the bridge between the unseen world and the seen one will reveal itself to you. It will beckon for you to walk across it, to boldly express the things that press against your heart. To mold, bend, shape, color. To give form to something. To liberate the forces that dance below the surface, at the core of everything that is.

To start the creative fire, I will end this chapter by sharing with you one of my favorite ways to visualize.

Warning, though: this is some powerful stuff.

⇥ power exercise for ⇤
VISUALIZING YOUR CREATIONS INTO FORM

Preparing for the Exercise

Find a quiet, private space. Grab a pen and a journal.

Doing the Exercise

1. Start out by writing down what it is you want to create. Is it a play, a sculpture, a clothing line, a nonprofit organization, a tech company? What one thing is calling to your heart right now, demanding to be born? List all of the details, ideas, and flashes of brilliance that come into your head. This could be based on appearance, how you'd like your creation to feel, what elements your creation consists of. Anything that can help to shape or inform what this new birthing could look like. Go

crazy here and let it flow. Not all of these ideas will stick in the end, and that's okay. You're just now opening yourself up to the possibilities.

2. After you've described the many facets of this creation, of this dream, close your eyes. In your mind, start to build the picture of what this creation will physically look like. The words you wrote down might help you with this, or you might find that you go down another track entirely. Whatever feels right to you is always the best thing to run with. If you want to open up your own yoga studio, start to see the physical place. The walls, the floors, the doors. See the people coming into this space and filling it with warm, palpable energy. Dare to go there. Create that world in your mind. See it as if it were something that already existed. Paint the details of all things in the space.

3. As you stay locked in this visualization, feel into your heart space. Feel the sensation of your heart, totally fulfilled. Feel the creative energies there crackling with affirmation. Know, deep within, what it feels like to not only hold this vision, but to live it, as if it were really happening. And you know what? *It is really happening inside of you.* The world within is wrapped up in meaning and energy.

It is a vibrant plane of possibility. Don't take this world for granted. Soak yourself in it. Let the juices of it marinate within you. Once you start to believe that your inner life is just as valid and worthy as the one outside of you, then you will really begin to open up the possibilities. You will feel the energies of deep fulfillment, and these energies will attract you to the vibration of the thing you'd like to create for yourself in the outside world. Harness the feeling. Get lost so completely in your visualization that the feeling will spontaneously arise within.

4. After getting drunk off of this feeling, you can either go about your business, or if the time is right, start creating. If you start creating, you will feel the creative power within you. It will be moving full force, flowing through your hands and your heart and your mind. It's a refreshing joy to create from this place, when your energy, your vibration, is so high. Use it and you'll see!

   If you're unable to create after this exercise, then go about your day, anchored in the feeling of fulfillment. Stay anchored there, as much as you can. If you find it slipping, try to visualize your finished product again to spark the feeling. Once you have it, hook into it and stay situated in it throughout the day. This will keep you inspired. It will help to bring greater power to your creations, once you're ready to take action. It will also fill your mind with ease and help you to stay in the flow of thoughts that are nourishing and empowering.

That's all it takes. A little seeing and feeling. Opening up the mind, expanding the heart into what could be. Barreling through the endless space that has been waiting to be filled by you.

STAY PRESENT TO THE FIRE IN THIS MOMENT

IN LATE 2015, WHEN all the doctors said there was nothing that could be done to stop the fast-growing cancer that was spreading across my precious father's body, I dug my fingernails into my deep-rooted denial and squeezed as hard as I could.

This couldn't happen. I wouldn't let it. My dad was my everything. I refused to believe that he was dying. All of us in my family did.

I dropped everything to be by his side. I was teaching a weekly women's circle and seeing various clients at the time, but I slowed a lot of my work down to make room to support my dad.

I spent many late nights reading up on alternative cures. I became obsessed with discovering new anti-inflammatory recipes and smoothie concoctions that many claimed could cure cancer.

Twenty pounds shed off of my body in a matter of days, as I was so consumed by my denial, by my need to keep my dad alive, by my foolish belief that I actually, somehow, *could*.

But then, weeks later, we lost him.

I was by his side as he took his last breath. He was looking up at the ceiling, his eyes glassy, yet wide open in wonder. And then he was gone. Just like that.

I've replayed that moment in my head so many times. In that last breath, in that single defining moment, all of the resistance in me became dust. The denial that I had held on to so fiercely in my heart for so many weeks had evaporated.

It was a sacred moment, witnessing that last breath, being there with him until the end; this man who had been so instrumental in supporting and shaping the woman that I had become.

I had to stay present to that moment to really feel and experience it.

My dad's death was the worst thing that has ever happened in my life, but it has also led me down a path of deep transformation, more so than I could have ever imagined.

In life, we must accept the ever-changing nature of all things —relationships, preferences, moods, structures, jobs—to embrace what is.

None of us were meant to live in the past *or* the future. The present moment is where the magic happens. It's where the brilliance and boldness of your feminine strength lies. You must stay present in order to fully occupy the space that you are in.

In that moment, I had no choice but to accept my dad's departure. Staying present to his loss, especially as it was happening, was a gift.

I know I just used a very heavy example here. But whatever you may be experiencing, whether it's something completely life-changing or ridiculously mundane, you must stay present to the moment. This will keep the mind open and vibrant.

Being present means that you are here, now, in this moment. It means that your mind is clear; you're not dabbling in the low vibration that comes with entertaining disempowering thoughts or holding on to old constructs. When you are present, the past and future no longer matter to you. You're not operating in the confines of time anymore. You move beyond time. Instead, you start living in a world where possibilities bloom in all directions. You become a magnet for all the things that you desire.

Being present to my dad's death, and fully accepting it, opened up a wealth of healing, experience, and opportunity for me. I would give anything to have him back, but at the same time, I am honored to have had him as my father on this earth for as long as I did, and to have learned and grown so much from his loss.

Some of us feel powerless, based on the fact that we can't control the outcome of every little thing that occurs in our universe. But to truly know our power, we must live in courageous acceptance of this truth. Always remembering that we have the power to choose, in every moment, how we react and how we move forward. It's okay that you don't control every single piece on the board. You're safe. The universe is embracing you every step of the way, hoping that you will one day remember the beauty of all that you are.

Be present to each moment. It'll be challenging at first. We've all been so used to having our thoughts run on autopilot for so long. We've kept ourselves tethered to the past. And we've grown accustomed to taking in all the negative messages about our bodies, our capabilities, and our intelligence.

But we can move beyond all this. And how do we do that?

The answer: through the breath.

The Breath = Life

The breath is an integral part of who we are. It is the link between body and spirit. An energy that transforms and creates. And it will never lie to us. It will show us who we are in any given moment.

When we're not present, the breath will be shallow; when we're tense and stressed, it will be choppy and unruly; when we're angry or sad, the breath will be stifled; when we're relaxed and happy, the breath will flow freely and with ease; when we're in deep states of presence or meditation, the breath will be a dynamic, healing cocktail of rejuvenation and transformation.

And finally, when we cease to exist, the breath will be no longer.

It is the barometer of all that we are. And if we can learn to use the breath to center us and make us more present, it will do just that.

But here's the problem: Many of us don't have a deep and conscious relationship with our breathing. We take the breath for granted, because it's something that the body does automatically and usually without great effort. So we coast through life. We forget to breathe into ourselves. We forget that the breath is the spark of life, of all that we are.

The image-obsessed culture that we're immersed in doesn't help things either. When women are put under pressure to meet rigid body standards, they do things that might not be the healthiest or most comfortable.

For instance, many women, in aiming to achieve a slim waist, will hold their stomachs in. We'll actually put effort into tensing up the muscles of the stomach so as to appear skinnier and more lean. When we hold in our bellies, not only is it uncomfortable, but it cuts us off from our breath.

A full and deep breath should reach all the way inside, down into the depths of the belly, so that it can stir up your deeper energy centers within. When the belly is clenched up tight, however, the breath has no room to move and flow. It remains in the head, throat, and upper chest, which stimulates the energy in the mind area, keeping us from being in the present.

➤ *power exercise for* ◀
STAYING PRESENT

Preparing for the Exercise

This one can be done anytime, in any place.

Doing the Exercise

Whenever you find your mind aiming to detract you from the present moment, catch it. Then interrupt the thought with a big, deep breath.

Let the breath oxygenate your whole body; feel the tingle from top to bottom. This cleansing breath should feel as if it's massaging the entire body as it comes in and goes through you. Guide your inhale slowly, all the way to the end, without stopping it prematurely. Once you've reached the end of that inhale, do the same with the exhale. Allow the breath to be fully expelled from the body in a slow, deep release.

And continue this way. Inhaling and exhaling.

And say these words in your head: *I have a right to be here.*

Let these words be a declaration of your commitment to the present moment. Let these words be your battle cry, as you valiantly brave the new adventure that each and every moment brings. Let these words light a fire in you, affirming that your presence on this planet is sacred and divine. Let these words remind you of the goddess that you are, as the vibrancy of your being steps back into the *now*.

MEDITATE LIKE
A MINDFULISTA

BEFORE I STARTED MEDITATING, I didn't understand what the big deal was.

How could sitting there quietly lead to anything that would be worth my time? I had tried meditating before, in yoga classes, during Shavasana. I'd lie there, feeling all tingly after doing all the poses, and I admit, it was nice. But there was nothing beyond that for me.

When I truly started meditating, that mindset changed. I would sit there and get swept away. My physical body felt as if it were losing all boundaries, to the point where everything around me felt like it was a part of me. My heart started to vibrate with an unspeakable power. My mind sparkled with rays of sunshine clarity.

There's a word I like to use when I'm talking about badass women who are fiercely present: mindfulista.

A mindfulista is a woman who gathers all of her precious energy and channels it into making every moment a kind of blissful meditation. You can see it in her. She is in complete and total acceptance of every moment.

That's because when you meditate you're clearing the tangle of brush away, so that you can feel the power that is present within you. Multiple layers of reality are penetrated, while your subtle energies are summoned up to the surface.

This is of tremendous importance, in a physical world where the mind becomes easily fragmented. Our thoughts carry an obscene amount of energy. In fact, each thought is packed with so much energy that it has the potential to physically manifest experiences, things, and people into our lives. Whatever we choose to focus on becomes our reality.

Thoughts are electricity. They magnetize certain frequencies to us, depending upon what we're thinking. Allowing our thoughts free reign to charter across any territory whatsoever is a dangerous undertaking. Sprawling thoughts are inevitably going to veer into low places that will suck your vibration dry.

Worries, aggravations, plans, past upsets, negative beliefs, and doubts will elbow each other out of the way to get their chance to become the focal point of our attention. It's like having a television channel with sixty different shows trying to edge their way in to play during one single slot.

It's utterly impossible, yet it persists. On a daily basis.

Walking the Path of the Mindfulista

A mindfulista is a fearless woman who takes all of the armor off, just seconds before stepping out on the battlefield. Her battlefield can be a number of places—in front of her altar, on top of a cushion, out in nature, on a shaded rooftop or balcony. Once she gets there, she sits, heart open, shoulders drawn all the way back. She gives herself up to the present moment. Her breath and her body synchronize, and in the synchronization, she exercises her ability to erase any trace of time or space. She is infinite. She accepts herself as she is, and she surrenders to the ocean of mindfulness that flows, and sometimes rages, within.

If you approach meditation in this way, you will know the force of your power. You will feel yourself growing in accordance with the endless doors that are being cracked open within you.

It takes work to fan the thick flame of our thoughts. Time and energy must be strategically directed at nurturing the kind of mindset that will inspire us to never stop moving forward.

Meditation is the essential element in all this. At first, it won't be easy; any mindfulista is going to have to face some challenges head-on. For one thing, persistent thoughts will behave like leeches, latching on, even as she attempts to meditate and keep the mind free from disruption. She might also be met with boredom, discomfort, stormy emotions, anxiety, or just a simple, soul-screaming frustration that she's just not doing it right.

Every woman will know a different journey, but regardless of what it is, she must keep reminding herself to show up. Day after day. Setback after setback. Just show up. Resume the position. Close the eyes. Breathe the breath. And then look the present moment square in the face.

That's what it takes.

If you continue to do this, at some point, you will start to feel the clarity of your true, vibrant spirit. The flame of all that you are will reveal itself to you. It will be irrefutable. It will lock you in a tight embrace and shake the sleep out of your eyes. It will nurse you back to the truth that has been aching to be known by you.

→ power tips for ←
MINDFULISTA MEDITATION

Preparing to Meditate:

To know the benefits of meditation, you must put aside at least twenty minutes a day to practice it.

Make it a ritual—one that you pour every ounce of your being into each day.

Give yourself over to your meditation process as you would a lover. The breath, the body, and the mind must all surrender. The muscles must be loose and relaxed. Wear clothing that is comfortable, so that the belly and the legs are free and unrestricted. The temperature in the room should be just right.

Doing Your Meditation:

I say "doing" meditation here, but really, the meditation will be "doing" you.

Start your meditation practice with a big inhale, followed by a deep sigh that rushes out of you like a stream. Feel the weight of all things that press on your spirit being released in this moment. Feel the body centering.

And then begin to meditate.

Keep things painfully simple at first. Not so painful that you're bored, but in a way that makes it all doable.

The trick to staying consistent with your meditation is to not take on too much in the very beginning.

Make it a simple practice. Follow your breath in and out of the body as you close your eyes. And that is all you must do. There doesn't have to be more. As long as you can stay present to the breath, you're meditating.

If thoughts come up during the process (and they will), don't beat yourself up about it. Don't throw your hands up and walk away from the whole thing.

Meditation isn't about perfection. In actuality, going through an entire twenty minutes, or thirty, or forty, without a single thought is quite challenging, regardless of how long you've been meditating.

The idea is to shower yourself with love and acceptance. Even as a thought pops into your mind, accept that it happened. Then make the decision to come back to your meditation. This will take effort and discipline, but you'll get the hang of it.

When thoughts are pummeling ahead full force in the mind, that's a clue that you're not present. Instead of ignoring the clue, you've got to use it. Use it to remind yourself to breathe, to feel your body, to come back to the moment. That's a skill you can use outside of your meditation practice and take into your life as well.

Once you become more familiar with the practice of meditation, you'll notice that the thoughts will start to recede. There will be no more baseless chatter. You will start to hear the clarity of the deepest, highest parts of you. And there is no sound sweeter than that.

STOP ASKING FOR PERMISSION

REGARDLESS OF WHAT ANYONE says, *regardless of what you say*, the truth is this: you're allowed.

You're allowed to be who you are. To express yourself fully. To sashay across the room with wild eyes full of confidence.

You're allowed to be brilliant. You're allowed to be powerful. You're allowed to feel loved, respected, and cherished.

There is nothing standing between the woman you are now and the woman that you yearn to become. There is no wall to break down, no endless mountain to climb.

In many ways, who you are and who you desire to be are the exact same person already. The thing is, you've been pushing against the current. You've been burning all of your energy trying to become something else, or someone else.

But instead of trying to become, why not just be? Stop fighting what is.

The woman that you are is already fierce and powerful. She is already wise, stunning, present, and complete. Stop tangling yourself up in knots trying to get to where you want to go; that way, you can just be where you already are.

Where you are, right now, in this moment, might not seem very glamorous. It might seem quaint. Or drab and dull. Where you are might represent aspects of the self that you don't feel comfortable engaging with.

But if you can't be where you are, if you can't be who you are without constantly forcing improvements upon yourself, then you will never know the gorgeous depths of your being. You will always be running away from yourself. Creating new masks and new layers to cover up your truth. To fill up the empty space, where all things echo. Where the radiance of you shines through.

There is so much beauty to be found within you. Right in this moment.

You don't have to travel to sixty countries or build a multi-million-dollar empire to carve out some sense of importance for yourself. If you'd like to do those things, go for it—but don't let yourself be motivated to travel and create success just because you want to become someone.

Be someone now. And not just anyone. Be you. Come from that place—that rich, vibrant, sparkling place, where you are vibrating at your highest frequency. Get out there and impact the world.

Live like a woman who knows that she's allowed. Let the divine intelligence of your pure and precious being slip into the driver's seat. There are no excuses anymore. There's no time to sit in the stagnant waters of fear.

To release your allegiance to becoming, so that you can start being, you must unravel the spool of thoughts that keep the essence of who you are under wraps. This doesn't have to be difficult, and the journey toward liberating the mind doesn't have to take months or years. Yes, maybe you've been harboring these thoughts for a long time, but the unraveling of them can be done rapidly. With your intention and your presence, you can do anything. You can come back to the higher reality of all that you are and all that you encompass.

A Vast and Intricate World
Is Unfolding Within You

This higher reality is something that eludes the mind. The mind is caught in the trappings of time and space. It is not eternal. It does not understand the boundlessness of your being. It cannot fully realize the magnitude of your presence. It dabbles in the low vibration of fear. It keeps you from being, from completely embracing yourself as a *woman allowed*.

But you must get the mind on board, if you want to stay centered in the being that you are. You must keep the mind present and drenched in the energies of love, so that it has no use for concocting any other destructive thought bombs that might knock you off course.

So how do you do this?

You can try to throw positive affirmations at the mind, to drown out the sounds of chaos. This works for some people. But let's go deeper than that, even. Let's settle in on magnifying the feelings.

The worlds of feelings and sensations are portals to the divine. They must not be overlooked or ignored. These are all opportunities for you to expand, to see more deeply into yourself.

If you're driving in your car and you feel something fluttering in your heart, what do you do? Do you shake off the sensation and focus your mind on something else? Or do you investigate? Do you go deeper into the feeling to try to uncover what's there?

So many things happen to us at an unconscious level and we're missing out if we're not aware of them. The energetic wisdom of the body keeps us aware. Even though our conscious minds might not register something, the unconscious plays out in the body, where it can be felt. There is a vast and intricate world unfolding within us, one that is always reminding us of who we are.

→ power exercise for ←
BEING AND LOVING WHO YOU ARE

Preparing for the Exercise

Clear just fifteen minutes in your day to devote to this love-fueled exercise. Find a comfy and quiet spot to sit or lie down.

Doing the Exercise

There is an invisible bridge that exists between the conscious and the unconscious. Through this bridge, both aspects of ourselves are always in direct communication.

For this exercise, I want you to bring your palms together into a prayer position at your heart. As you hold your hands in this position, settle your undivided attention on the heart. And breathe.

Feel the mighty currents of love that travel in this space. Let all the muscles in your face, your shoulders, your legs, and your womb relax down toward Mother Earth. As you relax, allow the energies of love to overtake you.

And I want to say this: If you're not feeling anything here, or you find it difficult to concentrate, just breathe and let go of your disappointment. Come back to the breath and to the heart. Have compassion for where you are right now.

And try to spend a little time each day just breathing while you feel into your heart.

Eventually, you'll strike gold. You'll hit the mother lode, so to speak. You'll feel love and all its many textures. Let yourself sink into this feeling.

Set aside the time to reconnect to this feeling every day, and you will find your entire body and soul getting swallowed up by it. Love will pervade every part of your being. And it's the feeling of that love that will carry you.

That feeling will be so strong, so palpable, that the unconscious mind will drink it in. It will understand it as the new order of things.

And most importantly, it will communicate this to the conscious mind. Despite itself, despite its obsession with keeping you safe and comfortable, the conscious mind will be bursting with thoughts that drip with the frequencies of love. The conscious mind will start to shatter and eat away at the old inner assaults.

Then, gently, gracefully, like the queen that you are, you will slip into a state of pure being. There will be no more craning your neck, no more soul-crushing expectations, no more looking off into the distance, straining to find that moment when you will finally become someone of value and importance.

You are everything you yearn to be already.

Actually, you are more than you yearn to be. Way more than your mind can fully comprehend. Stop trying to become, and start being. Strip off the masks, the armor, the fears. Burn away all the things that keep you insulated. Draw out the center of yourself, the inner parts of you. Emerge from the smoke of illusion, raw and awake.

As you are.

As you always have been.

⇒ *affirmation of* ⇐
WORTH

I am worthy.
I know my worth.
I feel my worth.

I am worthy of this body.
I am worthy of this heart.
I am worthy of this soul.

I am worthy of happiness.
I am worthy of peace.
I am worthy of love.

I am worthy of pleasure.
I am worthy of joy.
I am worthy of abundance.

And I have a right to be worthy.
To know my value.
To walk with confidence.
To feel my worth radiating within me,
Like a thousand suns.

⇀ badass self-care for ↽
THE MIND

The definition of self-care is yearning for some serious expansion.

Caring for the self is often limited to things like soaking in a hot bath or getting a manicure or massage.

And although I'm not saying you should cancel your upcoming spa wrap, I do feel that we need to look at other alternatives that might help us to forge an ongoing relationship with self-care. We should find a new way to practice self-care, one that isn't solely reserved for an upcoming appointment and doesn't require much effort to bring into play.

A way we can begin to do this is through the mind.

Your mind needs ongoing self-care, just as all other aspects of you do. But the mind often gets overlooked.

The mind is the starting point where all ideas and beliefs curl their way into form. It's from the mind that our words and actions achieve lift off.

The mental world is what imagines and shapes the outer world into being.

In my opinion, it is essential to engage the mind in as much focused and intentional self-care as possible. Only then can we elevate our inner landscape so that the outer one can rise to match its vibration.

⇢ *badass self-care ritual for* ⇠
THE MIND

Preparing for the Exercise

Plan for a day when you will consume no negative or distracting information that might weigh heavily on the mind. This means no television, no news, no social media. No texting, even.

Doing the Exercise

Unplug from all sources, so that you can just be.

Your mind doesn't need any more information or stimulation. It doesn't require Twitter or media channels to fuel it with power.

In fact, all of the information detracts from your power. It leaves you cloudy, unfocused, caught in the loop of wanting more and more, yet never getting fully satiated.

So let it all go. Take a day to allow your mind to rest. Give it a chance to breathe, so that you can truly stop and hear yourself. There is so much noise and chatter coming at us from all directions. And although it might be unrealistic to completely unplug from everything 100 percent of the time, we can build in a day here and there for not feeling pressured to constantly pursue more information.

Taking the time away from all these sources will also make you truly understand just how much fear is being perpetuated with all the content that is being shared and created.

The mind can tap its own natural vibrancy and clarity, without taking in all the fear-based media and posts.

After you've gone a whole day doing this, try to take this wisdom into your daily life. Recognize when you are caught up in social media, scrolling through like a zombie, eager to consume more and more content. That way you can take a break and step back from it. When you're watching something on the news that is filling your stomach with dread and tension, make note of that. And turn off the television.

You have the power in you to do this. You can practice this badass form of self-care for the mind on a daily basis and you'll be a stronger woman for it.

SECTION II
→ BODY ←

A note: *I want to add that if I'm mentioning the breasts, the womb, or vagina in this book, and you don't have one or more of those parts, this never means that you can't access the same power. In this case, for breasts energy, you plug into the chest area; for womb energy you go just below the navel; and for vagina power, it's all about accessing the pelvis/genital area. Whatever body you have, fierce woman, know that it is beautiful and powerful and will offer you access into the wonder of what you are!*

BECOME MADLY DEVOTED TO YOUR BODY

YOU ARE BEAUTIFUL. EVERY inch of you.

Every curve, every line, every so-called imperfection.

You are the physical embodiment of the universe's longing to know itself. Every part of you was born out of love, and so you are naturally love itself. Do you feel that?

You are a physical goddess. No matter your color. No matter your features, weight, or height. No matter how much your body has changed, whether it's a result of time, pregnancy, or stress.

You are simply, divinely the expression of perfection.

The way you move reflects the electricity of oceans. The features on your face reflect the sacred lineage of strong women that came before you, and that you are an integral part of. The lines on your hands, the way they reach and grasp—see the beauty in this. See in them the hands of the women who bled, raged, and loved before you. It's all there if you look. If you can just breathe and melt into your body, you will feel it. You will have a deep knowing. For your body is the articulation of the goddess that resides in every woman.

However, in order to feel into this, you must honor and accept your outer landscape. You must become madly devoted to all parts of your physical being. You must resist the urge to accept only specific aspects, like your eyes and arms, while you dismiss all the other parts of you.

Hierarchy has no place here. You must wrap your arms around yourself, in total, and love it all.

Will it be downright terrifying? Will you feel silly? Self-conscious?

Yes, yes, and yes. But it will all be worth it.

The constructs of the patriarchy have thrown a massive amount of energy into objectifying the female body, instilling deep shame, guilt, and pain in so many women. Instead of encouraging a woman to know the sacredness that is her physical form, culture has cheapened her connection to herself, leading her to believe that her worth is tied up in superficial aspects of how the body "should" look. And once women get caught up in this myth, it becomes a great challenge to embrace the beauty that is naturally present in the body.

This is simply something that must stop. Women everywhere must do everything we can to break the cycle.

If you can stop being numb to your body, if you can stop focusing on all the ways in which it fails to live up to shallow standards of beauty, then you will experience true fulfillment. You will know who you are. You will taste the sovereignty that every woman on this planet deserves to know.

Don't buy into the illusion. Don't get tripped up by the marketing of advertisements and commercials, the ones designed to make you feel like you don't measure up.

Because seriously—what is it that you need to measure up to, exactly?

You are beyond compare. There is not another body like yours and there never will be, in all of eternity.

Breathe that wisdom all the way in and wield it like a woman who knows her worth.

Beauty is your natural state. It cannot be otherwise.

Your body is the sacred container for your soul, which is always yearning for more expansion. The soul cannot expand without the body. It cannot go off on its own to do the work of self-love and acceptance. The body must come with it. And so, when you seek to grow your being, to open up to life in deeper ways, never neglect the body. It is your vehicle for expression and transcendence. It is a monument of feminine divinity that deserves to be cherished, and if you look the other way when it comes to this, you will feel a sense of lack.

Cherish your body now, because it will only last for so long. Once it dies, it's gone. Your soul will continue the journey beyond this life, but all of the lessons you could have learned—and the experiences you could have had—in this very precious body will be no longer.

Don't wait on this.

Body love is the deepest spiritual practice there is. One that you can start right now.

→ *power exercise for* ←
CULTIVATING BODY LOVE

Preparing for the Exercise

This exercise requires standing and movement. However, if standing is difficult, you can do this sitting in a chair or lying in a bed. If a little movement isn't too challenging, you can gently move the top half of your body from whatever position you're in.

Or, if you are not very mobile, you can subtract the movement from the equation and just focus on the breathing and the affirmation.

Doing the Exercise

Put both hands on your hips.

Inhale as you lean to the left.

Then, as you hold the stretch and your breath, and you look up to the sky, say in your mind, *I am a divine creation.*

Exhale and come back to center.

Now move in the opposite direction; same general idea. Inhale as you lean to the right.

As you hold the stretch and your breath, and you look up toward the sky, say, once again, in your mind, *I am a divine creation.*

Exhale and come back to center.

Keep repeating this, on both sides.

Continue for about five minutes.

When you're finished, bring your palms together at your chest and just breathe here.

Feel all of the energy and vitality of the goddess that you are radiating throughout your being.

Try this for five minutes each day.

It will help you to feel into the power of your feminine body.

HOW TO START A REVOLUTION AND CRACK THE CODE OF YOUR SHAKTI

THE FIRST TIME I experienced the feeling of Shakti running through me, I felt as if my body had been plugged into some universal light socket. There was this charge of electric fire moving within me. It felt like bliss-infused lava melting across my cells, filling me to the brim.

I became dizzy with ecstasy. I never knew that it was possible for the body to have that kind of experience.

That was ten years ago, and I haven't let go of that feeling since. I've liberated my Shakti and I keep her flowing through me daily. It's like having the taste of some exquisite nectar lingering perpetually on my tongue. Nearly a decade later, I still can't believe how intoxicating and powerful this energy feels.

It felt like I had been living in the walls of some stuffy room all my life, and finally a window had been opened, allowing a rush of air and light to flood in.

This is a great challenge, fully conveying a feeling so mysteriously sacred into words. *But you will know it when you feel it.*

Once you awaken Shakti, you will begin to understand how she moves and operates.

Your body is like a cave, overflowing with countless treasures.

Your every cell is a diamond. Your every atom contains within it a myriad of blessings.

Feel the way your heart beats within you. The way your muscles soften and clench. The harmony in the way your organs vibrate and regulate. Your body is alive; it is a wild jungle of intelligence. And it is available to you at all times. It is your power source and your wisdom war chest; it is proof that all things are imbued with a force that is devastatingly sacred.

As a woman, you are a garden bed of fierce potential. Millions of seeds are tucked into the contours of your soul. Harness deep inner awareness and these seeds will grow. The layers of fear will be stripped away and the goddess in you will be activated.

To activate this goddess, to kick the feminine power within you into the highest gear, you must do the thing that will turn your world upside down and inside out.

You must get cozy and familiar with Shakti energy.

What Is Shakti?

Shakti is the all-powerful feminine life force energy. This energy exists in the universe, and you also have it in your body. When you learn how to awaken it, you basically get an all-access pass to your highest self. To be in your Shakti is to be your most creative, vibrant, magnetic, sensual, and passionate self.

Shakti wakes you up to your own brand of magic. It puts you in deep communion with all the divine parts of you, which actually means *every part of you*. Cause there's nothing about you that isn't divine. There's nothing about you that isn't deserving of love.

Shakti reminds you why you're here. It drenches the body in a kind of warm electricity that gives you no choice but to wake up to your brilliance. Because sometimes it's good not to have a choice. Sometimes it's good to go with it. To trust that the goddess has got your back at all times.

In Sanskrit, *Shakti* translates to "sacred force." Sacred texts on Shakti can be traced back to ancient India. Tantra, which is a practice of embracing the oneness of all things, is based on an understanding that there are two principles at play in the world—Shakti and Shiva. Shiva is the masculine principle, while Shakti embodies the qualities of the feminine. Both of these energies are required for the well-being and balance of our universe.

Since our world has embraced a toxic dose of masculinity, it's no wonder that there is so much unnecessary suffering and destruction on our planet. When we grab hold of the feminine power, the Shakti, in our own bodies, we transform not only ourselves but the world as well. We amplify our own voices and our own light, and this inspires the women around us to let their voices be heard and their lights be seen as well.

So what you're doing here, with this book, with your intentions, with your sacred life—this isn't just for you. All women are in this together. All leanings toward competition must be dropped so that we can co-create a world that is based on audacious love.

Shakti is your pathway to this. It is home, because it is the essence of all that you are. It cannot be seen by the naked eye. But it is there, beating in sync with the rhythm of your heart.

How She Flows

Just as blood and lymph flow through the body, so does Shakti. It is life force energy that runs through the energy channels of your subtle body.

The subtle body is very different from the physical body. It is your connection to the realm beyond the physical. It records every thought, every feeling, and every emotion, regardless of whether you are consciously aware of it.

Within the subtle body are energy channels. Shakti runs along these channels. If your energy channels are open, allowing for the energy to run freely, you will feel balanced, healthy, confident, and fully expressed.

If your energy channels are blocked, impeding the flow of Shakti's journey through them, you can feel anything from depleted, worried, unfulfilled, and anxious to dissatisfied, down, stuck, lost, aimless, or moody.

So you might be wondering a couple of things. How do you know whether or not your energy channels are stuck or blocked if you can't even see them? And is there any real way to measure this kind of thing?

If you're just beginning to grasp what Shakti is for the first time, it can be difficult to comprehend. That is because this kind of thing isn't for the mind to understand. It's an experiential process meant to unfold in the terrain of the body.

Even so, you can start to forge a relationship with your subtle body. And just as you know you're hungry when your stomach growls, or you know it's time for bed when you feel your mind and eyes growing foggy, you will know when your Shakti is in her flow and when she's not. You will be able to measure Shakti by feeling just how liberated or cut off your energy feels.

When you're not allowing this feminine power to flow through you, it gets stuck. And Shakti never wants to be stuck. She wants to flow, not get pinned down or fixed to any one idea, frequency, or feeling for too long.

As humans, we often become too attached to things. We cling with all our might when we should be letting go. We treat change as if it were some kind of apocalypse, and we buy into the complacency of our comfort, and sometimes our discomfort, as well.

When this happens, our energy channels get eroded. And then we get stuck. We lose our way. These low points in life become difficult to navigate when we don't fully understand how to engage with and clear our own energy channels.

Think of Shakti as a long-lost friend who you would like to become reacquainted with. You might feel as if you are just starting to get to know her and that she is completely new to you, not a long-lost friend at all.

But, trust me—something mysterious will start to happen when you allow this relationship to go forward. You will start to connect to your Shakti in such a way that you'll feel as if you were remembering something. Your subtle energy channels will wake up a clarity of purpose in you that you always intuitively knew was there.

It will be like a breath of fresh air.

You will feel revived out of a long slumber of disassociation. And you will feel as if you've connected to some long-lost force that has been there all along, waiting for you to find your way to her again.

There is another life inside of you.

Your inner landscape is laced with crystal formations, ones that gleam through all of the wounds and heartaches that you have endured throughout this life. There is a beauty inside of you so lush that it would intoxicate you to the point of no return if you knew.

If only you knew.

Well, you can know.

To start activating Shakti right now (because why wait?), you can try this exercise right here.

⇒ power exercise for ⇐
ACTIVATING SHAKTI

Preparing for the Exercise

This one requires music and dance. If it's not possible for you to dance, turn on the music and lie on your back.

Doing the Exercise

Turn on some music that you know will get you into your sensual flow. It can be upbeat or slow; it doesn't matter. The important thing is that the music speaks to you, which will make it easy for you to completely surrender to this exercise.

Once the music is on, close your eyes. Start to breathe deeply through the mouth, connecting to your body.

Then start making circles with the body: the head, the neck, the hips, the arms, the legs.

Find all the ways in which your body can flow through circular movements. And make this into a dance. Allow all of the circles to come organically to you, as you flow from one circle to the next.

As you engage in this sensual circle dance, you must keep inhaling and exhaling through an open mouth. The breath is your foundation here. It will help you to go deeper and to really feel yourself fully.

Let this dance be a kind of meditation. Devote your heart and soul to it. Devote your full and complete focus to this very sacred act of making circles.

And mix up the size of the circles too. Make big ones, medium ones, small ones. Don't let yourself get stuck on a particular circle for too long. Keep the flow of the dance going as much as you can.

Feel yourself getting lost in this dance and allow the body's raw wisdom to take over.

Let your body move you, as opposed to you moving it.

Let it be spontaneous and free. Every moment of this dance should be full of ease and pleasure.

Keep this going for at least ten minutes. And if you're lying down and unable to do the dancing, you can connect to the breath and feel the music radiating in your heart. If you're able to, you can even make tiny circles up and down your spine.

You'll notice as you do this that it starts to open up your capacity for pleasure in the body. Our feminine bodies, hearts, minds, and spirits were made to receive pleasure and to know the full magnitude of our Shakti.

As you continue to read through this book, you'll find many other exercises within various sections, all for activating Shakti energy. You might find that you have naturally been doing things to activate Shakti your whole life; you just didn't realize it. Movement, yoga, singing, swimming, meditating, dancing, creating—all of these things help to awaken Shakti.

Now, as you do these things, direct your consciousness and intention into calling up this feminine life force so that you can summon up all of the latent energies within. As you continue to go down this path, as you let the knowledge of your feminine power seep into your cells, remember this: Don't push too hard. Don't strive like a madwoman toward quick results. Shakti will always elude you if you approach her this way.

Instead, stay soft and receptive. Some will awaken their Shakti quickly because it's ready. For others, it will take time. It doesn't matter when you awaken this life force within you. Just set the intention. Breathe. Feel your body more. Let your attention sink beneath the layers of the surface parts of you so that you can feel the life that throbs and pulses there. Everything will happen when it's meant to happen, and all is unfolding for you exactly as it should.

You've got this, goddess.

THE CHAKRAS HAVE YOUR BACK AT ALL TIMES

WHEN I STARTED OPENING my chakras, it was by accident.

I was meditating, locked in the grip of deep presence, when I felt as if the inside of my body was vibrating and spinning with deep joy. That was when I knew. That was when I got it.

It was as if a waterfall of sensation had been unleashed in my heart. I felt as if all the parts of me were expanding and all of the things that I had ever held on to unnecessarily were being washed away.

This experience rocked my world. It was one of the first times I really could feel that there was more to life than what the human eye could see and what the human mind could fully comprehend.

If you haven't experienced the sensation of your chakras buzzing, it might be somewhat challenging to fully embrace the concept of these major energy centers that work in coordination with certain aspects of ourselves.

I can honestly tell you that I never really gave chakras much thought whenever I read about them or heard the instructor mentioning them in a yoga class. It wasn't that I didn't believe that they existed. It was simply that the chakras held no real meaning for me. I had never physically experienced them at that point, and in my world, I need to experience something on my own before I truly understand what it's all about. Books and lectures have their place and serve as the catalysts for great transformation, but certain things are meant to be lived in order to be fully appreciated.

I like to think of the chakras as our panel of experts, each with their own unique specialty. It's a pretty badass concept, knowing that these seven forces have your back at all times and that you can never forget one of them at home or misplace them like a set of keys.

The chakras are always there for you; they always know where you're at and they will reveal this to you, minus the frills, if you can turn to them with your full awareness. They will do what they can to remind you, to gently align you back to balance and into your unapologetic wholeness.

Lose Yourself to Find Yourself

You are like a glass, filled beyond the brim. Overflowing with energy and sensation. Your entire body a whisper of some deeper meaning.

Unlock the trapdoor and slip into the space where all things ring with the tone of the indestructible. The potent fire within. Take refuge in this place. Feel all its textures—marry your attention to the totality of smooth and coarse, dull and sharp.

Lose yourself here. And through the losing, find the thing that you thought was forever lost. The highest part of you; the part that is the whole. That inexpressible soul essence, stretching across vast amounts of time and space, so effortlessly, to encompass all things.

The entryway to this place, the trapdoor that I speak of, it can be found in your chakras.

Chakra is a Sanskrit word meaning "wheel." It's a radiant disc of spinning energy that supports and fortifies various layers of our beings. All of us—men and women—have seven chakras in the body: root, sacral, solar plexus, heart, throat, third eye, and crown.

Each chakra corresponds to certain glands and nerve plexuses in the body. If you are experiencing any kind of imbalance physically in a chakra, that might mean that particular part of you is begging for your attention.

If your eyes are always stinging, your third eye might be out of its flow. If your heart feels weak, sad, and lost, your heart chakra is stuck. If your legs are endlessly sore, your root chakra needs your focus.

The physical body is always giving us clues as to what we need more of.

Also, the chakras work in deep coordination with your Shakti. The more clear and vibrant these energy centers are, the more alive and potent your Shakti will be. Working with the chakras is an essential part of understanding and taking back your power as a woman.

Here's a down and dirty chakra primer so that you get to know each chakra a little better...

The Root Chakra

The first chakra is located at the base of the spine. It's called the root chakra and it connects deeply to the ground, to Mother Earth.

This energy center represents stability, security, money, the home, and our connection to the primal aspects of ourselves. This is the energy that you work with when you desperately need to ground yourself and tame any other energies that might threaten to render you unstable. It's also the area to address if you're lacking in finances or the comforts of a happy home environment.

Clearing the first chakra will empower you to find your footing, feel stronger, and be galvanized by that deep connection to earth and nature.

The Sacral Chakra

The second chakra is located two inches below the navel. This is your sacral chakra.

In a woman, it's a place of pure power that should never be overlooked. This is the home of creativity, sex, and emotions. Liberating this chakra connects us to our pleasure and sensuality. It provides us with the strength to face our emotions with grace and acceptance so that they don't get the better of us.

This chakra stimulates the understanding of this deep dance that every powerful woman is an integral part of: the dance of light and dark. The courage to embrace both sides of the coin, no matter how aggravating or upsetting it may be. Freedom comes rushing in when we are open to the wide spectrum of emotions that exist. We start to build that muscle as we acknowledge that life is entangled with everythingness, and that to extract the uncomfortable from the equation is to live only a tiny portion of the human—and the feminine—story during this lifetime.

Plunge deep into unifying this chakra with your entire being if you want to learn how to navigate tough emotions, experience pleasure flowing freely through you, banish guilt and shame from sex, and step into your creative genius.

The Solar Plexus Chakra

The third chakra is the solar plexus chakra. It's located right below the ribcage, in the solar plexus area.

This is the home of ego, determination, and confidence. It's the fire of your ability to take action and blaze boldly ahead with confidence. It's the place where you work to develop a healthy sense of your self, because having an ego doesn't have to be a negative thing.

Having an ego means keeping yourself safe and protected. It means having the strength to reach in and pull out your courage whenever you need it. Working with this chakra will spark something in you, emboldening you to feel your power unapologetically.

Here's the thing about these first three chakras: they're usually not as developed in women as they are in men. This is due to the way that society "sees" men.

Men are typically seen as being stronger with the first chakra (ability to make money and provide), the second chakra (sex), and the third chakra (self-confidence, action-taking). Of course, every single person will be different and men by no means have these three chakras "in the bag." A lot of masculine energy is tied up, for example, in pushing aside emotions (second chakra). But men naturally are known to feel and work with the energies of the lower chakras.

What does this mean for us women?

It just means that we've got to turn this thing on its head. We've got to reclaim connection to these lower three chakras and create a strong foundation for ourselves, which will not only empower us but also connect us to men in a fluid and tangible way.

For example, in regards to the lower chakras, women are dominant figures in the area of the home (first chakra), and also the ability to express emotions (second chakra). So we do have power there that is waiting to be sharpened, but we must take that power and sharpen it away from the limiting frame of what culture tells us a typical woman should be like. Some women have no desire to tend to the home and raise children, while other women find it tough to let their emotions freely flow. The chakras are all about mixing up preconceived notions so that we can feel into what already exists naturally within us.

Our patriarchal society has shaped our world into believing (and perpetuating) very limited constructs about each gender. Our unconscious has wrapped itself around all of these limiting ideas of what and who men and women truly are, and we naturally start to play these ideas out in our own lives, whether we mean to or not. That is the power of culture. And though culture has its connective perks, we can't let it distort what's real and true.

The Heart Chakra

The fourth chakra—the heart chakra—is the home base of woman.

It is her own magical bunker—one that is secretly embedded in the middle of the war zone. It is the sparkling ember that glows within, situating woman, drenching her in the force of love that she is. This is the energy center of connection, empathy, immunity, and compassion. This love center beats with such excitement in every woman, compelling her to act, move, be, and do from a place of deeply contagious joy.

Settle into the heart and you will feel that sense of self-love burning within you; you will also feel greater connection and fulfillment in all of your relationships.

The Throat Chakra

The fifth chakra is the throat chakra. This is the center of communication and expression.

When you want to speak your deepest truth, feel into this space. Let your throat be activated with the powers of love and intention.

Women have the desire to communicate always, to connect and form bonds through words. We want to be heard, and we want the people in our lives to be heard. And so this space doesn't just encompass speaking; it is also about hearing the truth of others. Activate this center to find power in your own voice and be the fullest expression of yourself.

The Third Eye Chakra

The sixth chakra is the third eye chakra, located between your eyebrows.

This is the place of total intuitive power, psychic abilities, and the ability to "see" beyond the confines of the five senses.

Women are often heralded for their intuitive powers, for having feelings and visions of unexplainable knowledge and actually allowing themselves to be guided by those feelings and visions. If you embrace this aspect of yourself fully, you will be more deeply connected to your inherent nature as a wild mystic.

The Crown Chakra

The seventh chakra is the crown chakra. Situated at the top of the head, this is the place that connects you to the power of the divine.

Imagine that the crown contains an energetic chord that extends upward and connects to the otherworldly realm that exists beyond this one. It is that feeling of being tapped in and connected to something greater.

Connect to your crown chakra to know that you're not alone, to feel that stirring sense of oneness with all things.

Each chakra holds so much power and wisdom, and this is something that's available to you at all times. Wherever you go, you take this energy with you. You are never without your power. Nobody can strip this from you. Nobody can take away that connection to the natural energy that we all contain within.

Women naturally have more connection to the upper four chakras—the heart (love), the throat (communication), the third eye (intuition), and the crown (transcendence). Again, this doesn't mean that men don't have all of these abilities to connect, just that they are associated with the feminine and have been ascribed to women.

Ideally, every human being would be fully balanced in their chakras. This would bridge the gap between not only the conflicts of each individual's life, but also the conflicts between men and women, or masculine and feminine.

Chakra cultivation is a beautiful and sprawling science. It encompasses the self and the energy beyond the self—the energy that is greater than, yet contains what we are. There is no limit to this energy. It is an ever-expansive, ever-blooming flower that grows infinitely. Once you start to lock in to your natural power, you can work to cultivate and expand it.

⇥ power exercise for ⇤
GETTING YOUR CHAKRAS UNSTUCK

Preparing for the Exercise

This exercise involves placing your hands over the chakras and using words to amplify their vibration. Be sure not to place the hands directly on the chakras, but hold them just a few inches away from each one.

Sit somewhere that is comfortable and free of noise. Keep the spine straight and the shoulders relaxed.

Doing the Exercise

1. Root: First, place your hands in front of the root chakra, just a few inches away from it. With deep intention, as you focus on your root chakra, say the word *groundedness*. Now pause a moment to feel the energy of this chakra. Then say the word two more times in this same way. When you're finished, move on.

2. Sacral: With your hands over the area that is two inches below your navel (remember: don't touch, hover!), focus and say the word *pleasure*. Stop and feel the power of that word in this area of your body. Repeat two more times, and continue to the next one.

3. Solar plexus: Continue on and use the word *power*.

4. Heart: Continue on and use the word *love*.

5. Throat: Continue on and use the word *expression*.

6. Third eye: Continue on and use the word *intuition*.

7. Crown: Continue on and use the word *transcendence*.

Be sure to feel into each chakra without any kind of expectations. Just show up with your presence. You might start to feel a hint of vibration and resonance happening in each chakra. You might feel sensations of warmth or tingling. But if you don't feel any of these things initially, that's perfectly normal. Since your body isn't used to engaging in ongoing chakra work, it might take a few times doing the exercise in order to really start feeling what exists there. Stay patient and loving with yourself throughout this process.

And know that creating this kind of container will help to liberate each chakra into its fullest expression.

Words contain great energy within them. Using this energy in combination with that of your chakras will set up an exciting foundation for the feminine power in you to flourish.

YOUR BODY IS A VEHICLE OF ACTION AND EXPRESSION. RIDE IT.

THE GREAT DANCER AND choreographer Martha Graham once said, "The body says what words cannot." In her work and life, Graham never shied away from liberating and expressing her feminine power, her Shakti. She used her body as a tool for expression, something that was very controversial at the time.

Graham wasn't concerned with upholding the trend of safe dancers who erred on the side of graceful, delicate movements. She was looking to connect below the surface. She wanted to get to the root of things, no matter how imperfect it looked. This is why her critics were appalled in the beginning, calling her style of dance "ugly." They just didn't get it. It was too unabashedly confident, too oozing of feminine power.

But even with the naysayers, Martha Graham succeeded in becoming one of the most influential dancers and choreographers of all time. It's because she dug into her Shakti and never looked back.

I love this story because it shows how necessary it is to become fluent in the language of your body. As a woman, your body is one of the most empowering forces that you have at your disposal. It is the container of your inner feminine energy. Without it, you'd be unable to move, create, connect, shift, and grow in the ways that your soul requires.

Too many of us disconnect from the body completely. We've gone through so many setbacks and heartaches that we've become numb to the body, preferring not to feel what's there. We believe that by disconnecting or becoming numb we can preserve what's left of our sanity. We think that by cutting off our connection to what we're feeling, we can avoid future pain.

But let me tell you: this only prolongs it.

For countless centuries, the world has known of the power of women and their bodies. When women are connected to their bodies, when they are in direct relationship with their sensuality and emotions, that is when they are at their most powerful.

A woman's body encompasses the power of a thousand tigers. It is like a wild, rushing stream, flowing full force without obstruction. It is the very first burst of sunlight that pushes the day into its beginning.

The cycles of life and death are encapsulated in the body of a woman. The power of potential—what can be created and what can be destroyed—is present in every goddess: in the way she moves her hips, in the way she straightens her spine or cranes her neck.

A woman's body is both the starting point and the ending point—and all the infinite space surrounding those points.

Within its tissues, it carries the pulsing of emotions and intuition. It is a rhythmic database of wisdom and illumination. To unlock the mysteries of a woman's body is to unlock the mysteries of life itself.

Don't Get Stuck in Your Head

So many of us neglect to acknowledge and learn the wisdom of our bodies on a daily basis. Instead of succumbing to our inherent sensuality, we deny it. We don't see the value there. Instead, we put far too much of our energy into utilizing the powers of the mind, which is a very masculine way of operating.

When you're only relying upon the mind to live, you become fixed on logic, reason, and analyzation, often to the exclusion of everything else.

And women weren't built this way.

We weren't built to be mind-based creatures, relying solely on information and getting ahead. Of course, all of us require the use of our minds. We need the mind to think, solve problems, and follow steps. But that's not the only part of you worthy of steering the ship through the waters of your journey. You need the body to fully feel and shine your feminine power.

When you disconnect from the body and let the mind rule, you risk losing that connection to your inner fire. You lose the spark of the deeper reservoirs of intuition, that sense of wild feminine knowing that all of us have deep in our bones.

And you deserve to know the power of your body. You deserve to use it as a vehicle for expression, for love, for peace. You deserve to take your desires and to see them materialize into physical reality. And your body can help you do this.

Your body can grant you access to the unstoppable life force you have within you. It can support you in creating and embodying the reality that you crave for yourself.

The goddess within you can only wake up if you wake up to the expression in your body.

It's easy to do this. You can start doing this a little each day, and soon it will become as natural as breathing to you. You won't even have to consciously think about it.

⇒ power exercise for ⇐
MASTERING YOUR BODY

Preparing for the Exercise

You can be in whatever position is most comfortable for you. Anything goes.

Doing the Exercise

One of the most effective ways to start connecting to your Shakti is to be still.

So be still now and notice what's happening beneath your skin. Don't look for any explanations at first. Don't judge what you find. Just be still with it and notice.

If you feel anything in your body—discomfort, tingling, twitching, maybe the feeling of your stomach turning or your heart sinking—focus like a laser beam on that feeling. With every exhale, imagine that feeling expanding out from the place it's contained in. The more you exhale, the more that feeling grows, spreading throughout your entire body. Once that feeling encompasses every particle of your body, just breathe here and feel whatever it is you're feeling radiating across every cell.

Just be present to this feeling and see if it has any wisdom for you. It might be calling you to move and sway. It might be calling you to dance, or cry, or take action on something you've been long neglecting. The trick is that you're listening to your body without your mind telling it what to do. You're allowing the vehicle that is the body to move you, to propel you toward the next moment.

And if you don't feel anything? Not a problem. Relax and try again. And if you get frustrated, just stop the exercise and come back to it tomorrow. Your Shakti will still be there, waiting for you to notice the power that she is, that you are.

Extra Badass Tip:

Take this exercise out into the world. Be aware of your body throughout the day. Feel the body as you walk through a crowded room. Even as the chatter and activity swirls around you, harness stillness within. Become aware of what's occurring inside of you, even if you don't completely understand it.

Find stillness and feel your body at the store. Settle into bed at night and feel the sensations in the body as you fall asleep. Feel stillness and awareness of the body when you're with your partner, or your kids, or your parents, or your friends.

It might be tough at first. Inner stillness might not flow the way you want it to. It might feel awkward and forced. And that is okay, at first. Anything that is new will feel like this.

But as you continue to develop more awareness of yourself, it will become easier and easier. And then you will start to understand what is happening there. What is present within. You will understand that a certain clenching in your left thigh indicates a feeling of sadness you're holding on to. Or you will understand that the tingling sensation in your heart indicates the radiant bliss that you feel. You will notice every rumbling and every softening. You will become a master of your own body.

But before the mastery, be a curious and dedicated student first. Learn your body inside and out. You must be brave enough to sit with the discomfort, with the frustration, with the disappointment. You must be like an aspiring composer, poring over Beethoven's compositions, aiming to follow the hints that lead the way to brilliance.

Your body is a great treasure. You deserve to know it in this life. The fullness of your expression is dependent upon that knowledge. And as you get to know this body that you are so fortunate to have, you must also start activating the dormant energies within.

Try to dedicate yourself to a practice of daily movement.

Too often, we get our bodies into very rigid patterns. We repeat the same tasks again and again, to the point of completely dismantling our connection to the body. Spontaneity must be embraced to bring back the vitality of the body. A dance class, a game of tennis, yoga, qigong, stretching—all of these physical acts have the potential to kick the body out of its slumber.

If you continue to move in the ways you're accustomed to, you will continue getting the same results in life. The same emotions, the same challenges, and the same patterns will continue emerging from all directions. (Yawn!)

Really, what's the point of all that?

Remember: Your life wasn't meant to be stuck in the same gear at all times. The goddess in you seeks fluidity. The goddess in you seeks an engagement with the flow, with ever-expanding growth.

It's time to untame the stuck parts of you. Let's keep going.

SENSUALITY IS POWER

THROUGHOUT THE YEARS, MANY women clients have come to me asking how they can learn to awaken their sensuality. To be honest, it isn't really that difficult. Sensuality is already there, pulsing within, waiting for the opportunity to announce itself. It exists in every woman like a fire. It's an energy within, a fierce cocktail of awareness and pleasure.

Sensuality has nothing to do with the way your body looks. It isn't how flat your belly is or how toned your arms are. Its definition cannot be found in wearing sexy clothing or carrying yourself a certain way.

Sensuality goes deeper than all that. It is reliant upon feeling, engaging, connecting, *deepening*.

When you take a breath and you feel the way that breath caresses the inside of your body as it moves down into your belly, that's sensuality. It's an activation of the senses that puts you in direct communion with the world inside and outside of you.

Sensuality is also:

- Feeling the juices of a nectarine dancing on
  your tongue

- Digging your toes into the sand and nearly
  feeling each individual grain as it comes into
  contact with your feet

- Being in the middle of a forest and allowing
  the sounds of nature to wash over you

- Pulling a shirt out of the dryer and taking a
  moment to breathe in its fresh, clean scent

- Allowing your eyes to fully take in the
  splendor of a full moon or a lover

As the senses take the lead, it is as if a kind of magic dust has been sprinkled all over you.

The world around you starts to crackle with a new kind of aliveness. You start to feel yourself more fully. A kind of passion takes over the body and you become a walking display of sensuality in the full bloom of its expression.

Sensuality is what brings that intoxicating swaying of the hips. It's what illuminates your eyes with a certain kind of charisma. It's what infuses your every move and glance with a captivating confidence that the ones around you cannot help but notice.

In this way, sensuality ceases to be a configuration of shallow aspects—like the sexy curves or the pouty lips. Instead, true sensuality animates what's there. It becomes less about how you look and act and more about what you are deeply embodying and projecting from within.

Regardless of whether or not your curves are seen as the culturally accepted (and severely limited) definition of "sexy," they come to life by way of you submitting to your sensual expression. Without the true embodiment of sensuality, there will be a lifeless and artificial quality. And you will feel a piercing lack of fulfillment gnawing away at you. Without the senses taking the lead, we lose all connection to our feminine power, to the world around and within us.

This is often the culprit when we experience a lack of passion in life. Where there is no passion, there has usually been a dulling down of the senses. Awareness has slipped and we are not seeing, touching, hearing, smelling, and tasting in the ways that allow the goddess within the space to step forward.

If you ever feel that your passion and your zest for living are starting to wane, the solution can be found in your sensuality. If you ever struggle with feeling not sexy enough—not young enough, thin enough, voluptuous enough, pretty enough, developed enough, curvy enough, tall enough, short enough, soft enough, firm enough—you've got to switch up your focus.

Remember: You are beyond compare. There will never be another body like yours and there never has been throughout all of time. This body that you are in is a blessing. It is your opportunity to get courageous and transcend the limitations of the patriarchal framework that would like to keep the essence of who you are on lockdown. You must stand in the power of your sensuality.

Start to forge a radical relationship with all of your five senses. Surrender to them with the faith of a goddess who trusts that the holy unseen higher powers have her back at all times.

View each blazing sunset as if it were the first one your eyes have ever seen. Devote yourself to hearing a song so fully that you become the song itself. When you're in the shower, close your eyes and meditate on each drop that falls against your skin.

You already know how to do this. You were created for this.

Your spirit was given this body so that you could know the richness of this physical life. You were hardwired for this. This is something you can't escape from. If you deny yourself your sensuality, you absolutely cannot know the true height of your power as a woman. The captivating and mystifying elements of you will be seen and felt by no one.

Your gifts will be buried.

Perhaps this sounds quaint and inconsequential. Perhaps enjoying a sunset here and there doesn't seem like it could have that much of an impact.

So let me make myself clear: The practice of sensuality should not be reserved for a sunset or two in a given week. It should not merely extend itself to your sex life or those times when you're walking in nature. If you're going to do this, do this all the way. Let it overtake you, like some kind of divine madness that you never want to recover from. Get drunk on the beauty—and yes, even the chaos—around you. Stay present and aware of it. This will increase your ability to flow and accept, no matter what gets thrown in your path.

You will become like a kind of warrior who walks on razorblades and rides on the backs of lions in her spare time. Nothing will ever again break you so completely that you feel like all hope is lost. Nothing—not even failure, heartbreak, grief, or despair—will kill your spirit. You'll stay strong through it all. You'll cultivate an inner power that will carry you through absolutely anything. And yes, all this just by reclaiming your sensuality.

Feel, smell, see, hear, and taste your way through each and every experience. Every time you do this, a new layer will get pulled back, revealing more of who you are, blessing your beautiful being with more power and light.

And to assist you on this goddess-fueled path, I've got some exercises for you to try out. Pick one (or all of them) and have a go at it…

⇒ *power exercise for* ⇐
DEEPENING YOUR SENSUAL SELF: FEELING

Preparing for the Exercise

Find a comfortable place where you can lie down on your back. Put a pillow under your knees if you need to.

Doing the Exercise

Allow your jaw to drop open slightly.

Very slowly, start to inhale through your mouth. And here's the really important part: as you inhale, feel the breath on its journey, all the way down through your body.

Feel the breath coming in. Feel it touching the lips, then the tongue, then the back of the throat. And as you continue guiding it down, feel that breath travel all the way down to the belly. Feel the way that it energizes and oxygenates you from within. Stay with it. Don't get ahead of it or behind it. Keep all of your focus married to that breath and push it all the way into the belly, feeling the belly expand with its power.

Next, it's time for the exhale. Exhale that breath, through the mouth, once again.

And the same as you did last time, feel that breath as it slowly caresses your body. Feel it moving up and out.

Continue breathing this way for five to ten minutes.

When you're finished, notice how much more present and alive you feel.

⇥ power exercise for ⇤
DEEPENING YOUR SENSUAL SELF: TASTING

Preparing for the Exercise

Plan to do this one during a meal. Be sure you have the space to do this on your own, without anyone sitting with you, as it requires your full presence.

Doing the Exercise

For your next meal, make a point to taste each and every single bite that you put into your mouth. And as you do this, allow no distractions. Try not to read, have a conversation, watch TV, or think about all the things you must do after you finish eating.

Just allow yourself to be present for each bite. And truly allow yourself to surrender to the tastes. Take your time chewing and enjoying all the flavors and textures in your mouth, against your tongue, against your teeth.

Notice how much more embodied you feel as a result of this! You might also notice that your food tastes unbelievably scrumptious.

⇥ power exercise for ⇤
DEEPENING YOUR SENSUAL SELF: HEARING

Preparing for the Exercise

For this one, you can sit or lie down. Whatever feels comfortable for you.

Doing the Exercise

Close your eyes and take a few deep breaths.

Then, try to play a game with yourself. See how many individual sounds you can notice outside of the room you're in. These can be sounds on the street or in a room next to you.

Once you locate a sound, don't move on to looking for the next sound right away. Instead, just stay with this one sound for a bit and really allow yourself to take it in. This can last for thirty to sixty seconds.

Once you're finished with one sound, move on to the next one. See what else you can find, and once you find it, just sit with it for a bit.

Keep going, just like this, until you've uncovered all of the sounds there are to hear.

Once you cannot locate any other sounds, the exercise is complete. Be sure to take a few breaths before you open your eyes. Notice how much more present you feel as you come out of it.

→ *power exercise for* ←
DEEPENING YOUR SENSUAL SELF: SMELLING

Note: For this one, if you use essential oils, be mindful of possible allergic reactions like rashes or other irritations. Please do your homework on any oils that you use.

Preparing for the Exercise

Grab some lavender essential oil or any other oil that you might have.

If you don't have essential oils, you can reach for an herb, a flower, or even a piece of fruit.

Doing the Exercise

Take your essential oil, herb, flower, or fruit and breathe its scent all the way in. (For the essential oil, you can simply open up the bottle and breathe from there. Or, if you prefer, you can put a couple drops on your skin. Be sure to use a carrier oil to dilute it.)

Get lost in the scent. Feel every bit of it coming in through the nose and allow it to fill your entire body. Let yourself feel as if the scent is the only thing that matters. Do this exercise for a few minutes.

➜ *power exercise for* ⬅
DEEPENING YOUR SENSUAL SELF: SEEING

Preparing for the Exercise

Get out in nature and find a tree that you feel connected to and want to work with. If you can't go outside, sit near a window and set your sights on a tree or large plant.

Doing the Exercise

Go sit in front of a tree and study it with your eyes, as if your life depends on it.

Notice every crack and indentation. Notice the base of the tree and the way it merges with the earth beneath it. Take in the beauty of the branches and leaves individually. Notice where the wind comes through and sets the leaves in motion.

You will have a newfound love and appreciation for the power and majesty of trees after this exercise.

➜ *power exercise for* ⬅
DEEPENING YOUR SENSUAL SELF: USING ALL THE SENSES

Preparing for the Exercise

This one also requires being out in nature. Again, if you can't, you can sit by the window.

Doing the Exercise

Go sit in nature. Look around you and fully take in the beauty of everything that you see. Do this for a minute or two. Then close your eyes.

Go through all of the other senses, one by one.

Take a couple of minutes to focus on each sense and let yourself discover what's there.

What can you smell around you? Find things to smell, one item at a time. Once you've fully taken in one smell, try to find another thing you can smell. And so on.

Do this with the other senses as well.

Once you've finished up, just sit there for a few minutes longer and breathe. Fully take in the moment and notice any sensations that come up in your body. You might feel the spark of sensuality starting to radiate inside of you.

One last thing: Remember that the art of sensuality must not only be limited to the exercises on these pages. This is just a kind of nudge to get you going. Ideally, you will set aside some time every day to practice sensuality, but you will also look for opportunities to bring it into your every moment.

We are never separate from our senses. They're always there, waiting for the opportunity to be experienced and explored. So use them whenever you can. Use them to get you deep into the marrow of every encounter you have during each day. You will feel yourself waking up as a result. You will feel all of the dust and illusion fading away. You will feel the forces of passion and pleasure getting their hooks in you.

You will fall in love with yourself and your life in a way that you never, in a gazillion years, thought possible.

YOUR BREASTS ARE YOUR SUPERPOWERS (TWO OF THEM, ANYWAY)

ONE OF THE BEST parts of my job as a tantric educator is that I get to work with couples. Harmonizing the energies of the masculine and the feminine requires deep trust, love, and patience. It's wildly fulfilling to witness a couple overcoming their challenges to fuse a bond that is tighter than ever.

One couple that I worked with was intent on bringing the spark back into their lovemaking. I had worked with them for several sessions, but nothing was quite clicking yet.

All that changed when I asked the woman about her relationship with her breasts. She told me that there really was none, that she never saw the value in that relationship.

I gave her some exercises to start to become more conscious of her breasts, to start opening up all of the energy that exists within them. She went home and tried the exercises. A couple of days later, she reported back. She told me that by tapping the energies of her breasts, she was able to access sensations and depths that she had never known existed. It was like she finally tapped the core of her whole, beautiful, vibrant self.

I told her to take these exercises, to take that feeling of connection to the breasts, and apply it to her lovemaking. Once she did that, she and her partner had the breakthrough they were looking for. That tiny adjustment worked wonders.

And beyond that, she was able to use this adjustment and apply it outside of lovemaking. The energy of the breasts is not meant to be kept under lock and key, used only for sexual purposes. The energy of the breasts is a rejuvenating one; it's what binds you to the feminine and to your wild, ecstatic nature. To situate yourself in that energy, and then to use that power in all you do, brings about tremendous results.

The breasts are an extension of your heart chakra, two lush flowers springing from your chest, dripping of cosmic nectar and the buzz of possibility.

Why are the breasts so powerful?

For one, every woman's breasts and chest area contain a great amount of high-voltage prana. Lines of energy cross and bend within your chest, your nipples, and your mammary glands. These lines of energy cannot be seen by the eyes, but they can be felt. Spinning, whirling, flowing. Like someone turned on the power to a billion watts of energy. It just takes tuning in and expanding your levels of awareness to access it.

Life Begins in the Breasts. Really.

They say that life begins in the womb. This is an accurate statement, but I'd also like to add that life's truest origins lie in the breasts. That is where the energy of love lives, and the energy of love is what sparks the forces of birth and creation.

The breasts exist in deep union with the heart. Loving them and fixing your attention upon the lines of sensual energy that exist within them has the power to shake awake the goddess that exists within you. Below the surface, your breasts are tingling with sensual feminine qualities, and they contain the river through which deep orgasm flows.

As a woman, your body is primed to naturally act from the qualities of compassion, connection, and intimacy. Your strength, every woman's strength, starts in the heart chakra. You are at your best when you are thinking, feeling, speaking, and moving from this place. In your truest and most authentic state, you are like a faucet that is overflowing, gushing with love. Spilling love in all directions. Tasting love in every bite.

The force of love is so great within us that we sometimes create, both consciously and unconsciously, stories about all the ways in which that love might be taken away. We do this in our allegiance to fear. We close up shop and ignore the vibrancy, the electric confidence of the breasts.

It's no wonder that so many of us don't even stop to truly consider all of the power and energy that is available there.

Right there. Inside of you.

You don't have to take a single step to find it. You don't have to hop on a plane and scour the planet for it. It's in you. It's available at all times. Pulsing and radiating below the surface.

This is energy that can be harnessed. That can be used to create, to make love, to accomplish our goals, to liberate ourselves from the clutches of every rigid expectation that would ever attempt to strangle the unique truth of what we are.

Please know that if you, for whatever reason, don't have breasts—maybe you lost them in surgery, or you're a trans woman, or you aren't cisgender and weren't born with breasts— you can still plug into this energy. Since the breasts are an extension of the energies that exist in the heart, you can melt into your heart space in order to bring these powerful sensations to the surface. So dive in and whenever you see me mention the word *breasts*, substitute the phrase *heart chakra*. And remember, when working with your heart chakra, don't just limit yourself to that small part where the actual heart itself is present. The heart chakra actually encompasses the entire chest, so you've got a lot of area to work with. Take advantage of that!

How to Make Love through the Breasts

When we make love, we tend to concentrate solely on the vagina, or yoni. We pump all of our focus and expectational fervor into the yoni, when in fact, the yoni and the breasts have a very divine relationship with one another. They are both a part of the same equation. Take the breasts out of that equation and the yoni will not be nearly as open, warm, or inviting.

If you instead submerge yourself in your breasts, allowing yourself to feel the pleasurable and palpable energies that are there, your yoni will automatically open, like a flower. There will be no forcing, no mental effort. Then, orgasm becomes ever expansive; it consumes your entire being.

The best way to understand this idea is to put it into action.

Make love through the breasts (or heart chakra).

Subtract your focus from the yoni.

Have no concerns when it comes to being wet enough, open enough, or turned on enough. Stop riding your expectations and instead settle into the all-encompassing energy of the breasts.

There's power there. And it will carry you. Trust in that, because it's your birthright.

Let the journey become meaningless to you. Exist in the now and be with the experience from the breasts.

Stay centered in the breasts by breathing into them, training the eye of your mind onto both breasts at the same time.

Breathing deeply will help you to get into this practice. It will help to situate you directly in your feminine knowing so that you are anchored so completely from a place of love and fire.

The yoni will gift you with her warmth and openness as a result of this. And you will awaken something deep and alive within you.

This is the truth of everything that you are.

Pleasure. Vibrancy. Aliveness. Passion. Endless possibility.

But all of these things become difficult to gather into our awareness when we're stuck pursuing a very masculine way of engaging with our breasts, our yonis, and our sex lives. The masculine way tends to neglect the deeper energies of love and pleasure, skating along the surface of a vast and infinite ocean.

When you perform from a place of expectation, denying the expression that is present in the breasts, succumbing to a structure that denies women the opportunity to experience pleasure in a deeper, more powerful way, you walk around feeling displaced. As if you've been forced out of the warm and glorious home of your body, disconnecting yourself from the wild ebbing and flowing of emotions, memories, and insights.

Do you really want to deny yourself of all that?

If you've been feeling displaced and disconnected from the power of your magnificent being, the breasts can lead you back home, whether that's related to sexual pleasure or not.

Throwing heaps of attention onto the breasts should not solely be reserved for when you're having sex. This is your life force energy. Your Shakti. This energy should be open and available to you at all times.

If it's only reserved for sex, it will never be the fullest that it can be. You've got to make love through your breasts during your every moment.

Then, every particle of your life will be drenched in love and power. You will find yourself in a deep state of intoxication by the mere raising of a hand up toward the sky.

Your body will feel alive, lit up by a force so deliriously resplendent that at times you will feel as if all of the universe is inside of you. Quivering. Waking you up to the wonder of what you truly are.

You Are Worthy. Your Breasts Are Worthy.

Pay attention to your breasts. Rub and massage them. Gaze at them in the mirror. Don't settle for ratty old bras; adorn your breasts with bras that are luxurious, that feel good to you.

Treat your breasts like they are something holy and sacred. Don't give them over to just anybody to touch or be rough with. Be conscious of who you let in to penetrate your heart.

You are worthy. Your breasts are worthy. They are like precious stones. Love on them a bit each day. Soak them in warm oils. See the beauty in them.

After some time, you will begin to notice a feeling within.

This feeling will be small at first. It will be like kindling a fire. You've got to pay attention if you want to know this feeling. The more you pay attention, the more this feeling will expand. It will spread across your breasts, your chest, your heart. You will feel it, like a wildfire. Emboldening your every aspect. And you will know the power you have.

Power cannot be simply mental. It cannot be found solely by expressing grit or staying positive or shattering preconditioned constructs by raising your voice. There is a place for all of that, but no, it doesn't just end there.

Power, true power, must be felt within.

It must marinate in your heart and soul. It must be liberated by movement, by awareness, by inner peace. By the courage that is found when one surrenders to love.

The framework of power as something selfish, unkind, loud, crushing, and unapologetic must be batted down. It must crumble, it must become dust. Because women are creating a new paradigm. We are moving out of the shadows. We are embracing our true selves. We are demanding to be heard, to be felt. We are linking arms. Dismantling misogyny and owning every marvelous part of who we are.

If it seems crazy to you that one could get to that place just by giving the breasts a little attention, then you must start experiencing this for yourself!

⇥ power exercise for ⇤
YOUR BREASTS

Preparing for the Exercise

Go into a private, quiet space and lie down.

Doing the Exercise

Be still.

Focus all attention on the breasts.

Let everything around them melt away: the back, the legs, the face, the arms and shoulders.

Let there only be the breasts.

Feel them from the inside, both at the same time.

If you can get still enough, you will start to feel a vibration emanating from the breasts.

Be very mindful of any kind of sensation that gets stirred up by this meditation. The key is to become aware. If you can do that, you will start to feel the Shakti that is present there.

Once you've uncovered it, surrender your attention even more deeply, even more precisely to it.

Finally, narrow your focus a bit. Put your attention onto the nipples, both at the same time. Be careful not to merely meditate on the surface or the outside of the nipples. Experience them from the inside, both at the same time, being careful not to get caught up on just one nipple, as this will dull the experience.

If you don't feel anything at first, don't get frustrated. Try this for at least ten minutes.

As you do this, and even long after you finish, you might notice a new buzz of aliveness streaming through you.

⇥ healing exercise for ⇤
WOMEN WHO HAVE LOST THEIR BREASTS

If you had breasts but lost them to surgery, this exercise was created especially for you, dear sister.

When a drastic change or a severe loss occurs within the feminine body, it feels as if there is a negation. Something has been taken, altered, removed. Driving us to suddenly know ourselves as less than complete, as if we are now resigned to a perpetual state of lack.

But this is not the case.

Regardless of the ways in which your body changes, regardless of the feminine parts you currently have or don't have, you are still whole and powerful.

Mourn the change. Grieve the loss. Give yourself time to heal and adjust. And when you're ready, come back to the power of what you inherently are.

Enough chitchat. Here we go…

Preparing for the Exercise

Lie down on your back and get comfortable.

Doing the Exercise

Take deep belly breaths. With each exhale, feel your body melting into the ground beneath you.

Now, focus on the space where your breasts used to be. Breathe into whatever sensation you feel there. Allow your breath to align and to soothe this space with its life force–giving qualities.

Next, feel the energies of the heart rising to fill the space that has been left empty. Imagine that the heart is expanding out beyond your body and that it is taking on the contours of new, more vibrant breasts. Feel your expanded heart as your breasts. Breathe in the wisdom of your truth, which goes beyond what your physical self can touch.

Extra Badass Tip:

Even after you've completed this exercise, spend the day walking around and feeling your heart energy spreading into your breasts. Allow that energy to heal, restore, and nourish you from the inside out.

→ *power exercise for* ←
WAKING UP THE SENSUAL GODDESS WITHIN THROUGH BREAST MASSAGE

Do this exercise to wake up the sensual goddess within.

Note: For this one, if you use essential oil, be mindful of possible allergic reactions, like rashes or other irritations. Please do your homework on any oils that you use.

Preparing for the Exercise

To prepare, go someplace private where you can lie down comfortably.

Make sure you have some oil that you can use to massage yourself. It can be a basic massage oil, or you can create your own by using a couple drops of essential oils; for example, lavender with a carrier oil like almond oil.

Note: If you don't have breasts, you can do this massage over the entire chest area.

When you're ready, dive right in…

Doing the Exercise

1. Lie down and make yourself comfortable. Take off your blouse and your bra, if applicable.

2. As you lie there, take a moment to close your eyes. Breathe deeply a few times, in and out of the mouth. Allow yourself to relax.

3. Next, take your oil in your hands and start to very gently massage the oil onto your breasts. Be sure to massage the chest as well, to encourage the energy to move freely. For this massage, you want to create light circles, spiraling outward. Make sure the pressure is not too firm as you do this. Take five to ten minutes here…or longer, if you're really feeling it!

And here's a big tip: You want both hands to be doing the same thing on each side/breast at the same time! You want to keep the energy balanced between both, and this will help you experience even deeper pleasure than you could ever imagine.

4. Next, place your left fingers on the left nipple and right fingers on the right nipple. Very slowly start to create circles on the nipple area, and continue to breathe through an open mouth. As you make these circles, do your best to focus all of your energy on the nipples. Give yourself up to the sensations that are being stirred there. Make this into a deep meditation of sensual awareness. Let this juicy part of the process go for as long as you need it to! You might feel some very deep orgasmic sensations start to flood into your body. If that's the case, go with it. Tune your attention even more finely to these sensations. Whatever you focus on grows, so allow the sensations to expand with your awareness.

   When you're ready, you can move on to the next step...

5. Next, take the left breast in the left hand and the right breast in the right hand. Continue to breathe deeply through an open mouth. Gently start to squeeze and release the breasts together, at the same time, and start to sync the breath with the movement. As

you squeeze the breasts, take a deep inhale.
As you release the breasts, take a deep exhale.
Do this for as long as you like!

6. And finally, rub your breasts, chest, and neck
   with your palms. The pressure can be firmer
   here, and not as gentle as your previous
   touches. Also, let the hands randomly brush
   over the body. The left and the right don't
   need to be doing the same exact things in
   tandem, as they were doing before.

Perfect. You did it, fierce mama!

Place your hands over your heart and thank yourself
for that breast massage! And then just lie there for a moment and drink in the feeling. Feel the powerful, sensual,
and erotic goddess that you are filling up your entire being and making you dizzy with some wild love energy.

SLIP INTO THE WISDOM OF YOUR WOMB

NOTHING IS MORE POWERFUL than a woman's womb.

The womb is a complete and infinite circle. It is a bridge, a portal. The fire codes of creation are imprinted upon its massive depths.

If a woman ever comes to question her abilities or her talents or her worth, she only has to look within. Eyes closed. Hands upon the belly, below the navel. Breath soft and unforced, as it syncs with the vibration of her inner cosmic ocean.

The womb is unapologetic. It sets the tone. Operates beyond the boundaries of space and time. Lives and dies, a million times, at the altar of its own sacred culture.

It is a tree with branches that stretch for miles, curving upward toward the sky, while drinking in earth's promise through its roots.

The womb is a door. It is the secret garden of a woman's soul, crackling with immense wisdom and the bloom of sensual velocity.

From it, all of life expands. The pulse of excitement and madness. The miracle of babies. The outpouring of music, laughter, and pain.

The universe is the ultimate womb; it is the mother of all wombs. And so woman feels a pull, always, to transcend. Her womb beats in unison with the universe's womb. At times, she feels a quickening throughout her cells and her blood. Rushes of clarity that put her in direct communication with her feminine power.

This is what it is, she thinks. *Here I am.*

But then, all too soon, that feeling passes. And she forgets. Only to recall it all again when she finds herself lost in things like nature, a book of poetry, music.

But the trick is to know it through all things. Especially times of chaos and confusion.

A woman's womb is her connection to her deepest gifts. She must nurture that sacred relationship by breathing deep into it. By feeling into its many mysterious crevices and contours.

The ecstatic drum of creation beats within her; she must do all she can to filter out the noise so that she can hear it.

→ power exercise for ←
KNOWING THE WISDOM IN YOUR WOMB

Preparing for the Exercise

Go somewhere quiet and comfortable. You can either sit up or lie on your back.

Doing the Exercise

Place both of your hands gently on your womb. Start to breathe deeply as you connect to this space.

Settle your intention deep within the womb and notice the life that exists there. You might feel a pulsing or some vibration. Whatever you feel, breathe into it. Allow this infinite sensation to gather all of your focus. Give yourself over to the mysteries of the womb and put everything else aside.

Keep breathing and feeling into the womb space. If you have a tough time feeling any vibration or sensation here, just relax and continue deepening your focus. The feeling will come when you're ready for it!

Try to do this exercise for at least twenty to thirty minutes. The womb needs your time, energy, and love to fully release and be known by you.

After the exercise, journal about any visions or revelations that came up for you.

→ power exercise for ←
WOMEN WHO DON'T HAVE A WOMB

If you don't have a womb, you can still benefit from plugging into the power that the womb symbolizes.

Since Mother Earth is the Ultimate Womb of All Wombs (that's right—the UWAW), use her badass power as your anchor.

Preparing for the Exercise

Go outdoors and lie down on Mother Earth; get on your stomach if you can. (If you can't get outside or if this is too difficult for you, you can do this on your floor or on your bed, with pillows cushioning you.)

Doing the Exercise

Start breathing deeply.

As you inhale, imagine you are pulling all her energy and wisdom up into your body. And as you exhale, allow her energy and wisdom to intermingle with your cells, your lymph, your blood, your tendons, your muscles.

Continue this for twenty to thirty minutes, if you're feeling comfortable and able to.

You might notice Mother Earth speaking right to you. And her words might not be typical words. You might just feel her. You might just notice the sensation of an invisible force fastening you to her core.

Whatever you hear, feel, or experience is exactly what your beautiful soul requires.

THE WONDER OF
YOUR BELLY

Do you know how powerful your belly is?

In Japanese, the belly is known as "hara," which is the center of life force energy. It is the place where power gathers. Martial artists focus on using the force that is present in the belly to empower their movements.

In the chakra system, your belly embodies your sacral chakra. This is the second chakra, which is responsible for your emotions, your passion, and your sensuality. When the energy in this area is liberated, you will know it. It will feel as if a light has been flipped on in the body, illuminating everything in its path.

The second chakra is a key area in which we can liberate our feminine power. It's the place where sensuality, creativity, and expression plot all sorts of juicy exploits. It's where you go to tear open the pockets of pleasure that have been stuffed away inside you for too long.

These are deep waters we're braving here.

This is uncharted territory. The kind that stretches out far and wide. Vast expanses of grays and blacks. Pathways full of thorns and obstructions. The fears you cannot bring yourself to speak of, lurking behind every corner.

I don't mean to get all dramatic here, but it's true. And you know what? Despite all this, your feminine power is as easy to claim as it is to take your next breath. It's about soaking your vibration with the deep intention of your heart so that you can set the force of your power free.

All of us have been taught countless ideas and belief systems that have strangled our fullest potential.

Someone must've figured out how effortlessly powerful women were. Centuries back, people must've said

> *No, this is too much power.*
> *We would lose control.*
> *Let's pretend like it doesn't exist.*
> *Ignore the sacredness of her hips.*
> *Drown out the noise of her voice.*
> *Avoid the deep beauty, pooling there,*
> *within her eyes.*
> *The holiness of her expression.*
> *The divine power of her form.*
> *The love that radiates from her every breath.*
> *Let us forget what she is, so that she*
> *might one day forget as well.*

And all the people who heard this nodded their agreement. All of them decided that the story of woman's inherent weakness must be peddled, that her strength and power must be locked away behind a concrete door.

And so woman forgot.

But now it's time to remember.

One of the most effective ways of reclaiming your power is honoring the belly that you have. The majority of women feel a dissatisfaction with the way their belly looks. It's not flat enough or small enough for their liking. Some women hold their bellies in when they walk, hoping to keep the illusion of flat perfection in full effect.

The problem is that when you're unhappy with your belly, when you struggle to manage and define its proportions, you are limiting its power. You are withholding your love for a very vital part of your body.

The "belly breath" exercise is essential for centering and stabilizing your feminine mind, body, and spirit. The belly breath is the game-changer of all breaths, especially for a woman. Breathing all the way down into the belly not only supplies the body with a soothing jolt of oxygen, but it also lets your belly finally chill the F out and soften for once.

The belly's aim is, always, softness. All power is squandered when you tense it, when you tuck it in toward the spine. Your body is feminine. The lines and curves and energies that make up your essence are geared toward ease.

In order to flow, you must be soft. You must love your belly and be soft.

Doesn't matter if you have an extra layer or two of fat there. Doesn't matter if the belly has been altered so much after you've given birth or gotten older.

It's perfect as it is. The roundness of it. The softness. The stretch marks. The dimples. The moles. The lines and creases. It's all divine.

The influence and wide reach of cultural norms and beauty standards have nothing to do with you. They don't speak to the soul. They don't account for the true, innate, and authentic power of a woman.

So stop looking outward for that approval. Stop denying your belly its brilliance. Stop looking for ways to suppress your magic. The more you placate and posture in this life, the more you will suffer. The more time and energy you will throw into the gutter and lose forever.

→ power tips for ←
LOVING YOUR BELLY

Honor your belly.

Accept it.

Breathe into it, like the kind of woman who is on a bold mission.

Feel your inhale caressing the inside of the belly, and as it does so, marvel at the power of it. As your exhale leaves the belly, use the opportunity to feel yourself releasing all of the distractions, all of the noise and dense energies that would like to hold you back and keep your inner fire a secret.

At night, before you go to sleep, place your hands on your belly and give it a gentle rub, tuning in to any and every sensation that makes itself known to you. Say to yourself, a few times, "My belly is beautiful. I love and accept my belly, just as it is."

As you say these words, feel the body softening and surrendering even more deeply. Feel the powerful goddess that you are finally coming up to the surface after many long nights of submersion.

WHY GROWING OLDER CAN BE AWESOME

———

I'VE HEARD MANY WOMEN say that as they get older they feel as if their entire body has "dried up." *And these are women in their forties.* They feel as if their passionate, vibrant qualities have been completely zapped from them, and they are looking for ways to recover what they've lost.

Some might say that this is natural as you age. But I feel like that mentality alone is what creates this disconnect in women who are looking to regain their vitality.

As women get older, they receive signs and signals everywhere, telling them that they aren't as valued or desired as they once were. The weight of these ideas impacts the body. It seeps into the unconscious and reflects itself physically. Women start to notice how much less "womanly" they feel, and they shut down.

Maybe I've just completely lost it, but I'd like to imagine something different for all of us women. Read these words with your heart and see if you can imagine this with me.

The World I See for All of Us

I see a world where the goddess nature of woman is known and beloved. In this world, every woman lives in defiance of all the forces that would like to bind and inhibit her essence.

She can walk down the street with ease. She can celebrate her body without shame or guilt. She can send her voice booming across the length of an entire football field just to hear the sound—the way it catches, the way it inflects and reflects.

She can take the thunder in her body and transmute it out from her heart, amplifying the lives of those around her.

This is what happens when a woman embraces her eternal nature, when she knows that she is worthy, no matter her age, no matter the number of wrinkles engraved upon her skin.

She dances with her power. She defies every expectation, every stigma, every dogma, every distortion, every lie, every attempt to cut down the beauty of what she is.

This is what I know is possible.

This is what I feel in my heart for us all. We do this work of rising into our power independently, but we also do this with the other women around us.

I long to see the day when all of us women rise up against the limited systems that have ensnared us in their empty politics. Let's remake our own systems—ones that are based upon the understanding that as we age here on this earth, we become more wise, more beautiful, more sexy, and more purposeful than ever. In this system, there is no defining and constricting what it means to be a woman. Let's create spaces where we are the authors and the creators of our own stories.

The world has been hungering for these stories for so long. Now, unencumbered, let us tear off the panels of the box. Let us feel the definition of who we are expand into infinite space.

Something to Always Remember

You are eternal.

Nothing can mar your essence. *The real stuff of who you are.* Nothing can change that.

You are like the stars in the sky. There is nothing to subtract or add to you; you are whole and complete. What lies in you lies at the core of nature, and of all things. You are the articulation of luminosity, simply too expansive to be pinned down by the construct of time.

As you age, in a physical sense, you might feel as if you are losing pieces of yourself.

The delicate features of your face start to shift. Extra weight, wrinkles, moles, and creases start to appear in places that were once so smooth and firm. The youth that felt as if it would last forever starts to seem very far away, a distant dream. Your head begins to throb with the weight of this reality.

Time is looked at as the opposition. You try to fight it. To maintain the illusion that you are one of the ones who time has not had its way with.

But here's the thing: When you're fixated on denying the fact you are constantly changing, your highest self—the deepest, wisest goddess in you—will feel the lie in its totality. And it will carry the lie in its energy.

You will be walking in public, trying to maintain the illusion, yet you will feel a vacancy inside. As if somebody has checked out. The room of your soul will be empty of all its contents. The purpose of the heart will be stripped down. The vibrancy of the inner life will be sanded away. The inherent potency of your magnetic feminine being will short out.

This is also true when you're not necessarily straining to maintain the illusion, but when you're getting stuck feeling sad or angry about the ways in which your beautiful body is changing.

Since time is queen on this plane, we must allow it to guide us through the cycles of life.

That involves aging and experiencing old age (if we are lucky enough to make it there). You must accept the ever-changing physical beingness of you. Accept it, because therein lies the opportunity to lean into your power and trust in yourself as a timeless goddess who just gets better and better with every passing moment.

Although youth will one day slip away from us all, the qualities of youth will forever be ours if we can stay open and accepting. The vibrant energies of lightness, adventure, laughter, innocence, and curiosity—that is at the heart of what true youth really encompasses. The qualities of youth, the idea of what the word *youth* holds—that's the thing that we're all truly after.

This is where you come in and take your power back.

Because youth doesn't own those qualities.

Youth alone does not lay claim to the act of being carefree. It doesn't have the copyright on discovery and excitement locked up. It doesn't have exclusive access to those awe-inspiring feelings of wonder.

You do. In every moment. With every breath.

As long as you keep your heart open to what's coming. As long as you embrace every moment that you get to live and breathe in this beautiful body that is yours and only yours.

Every Number That We Are Is Fleeting

Youth isn't the only gig in town when it comes to having endless possibilities at your disposal. No matter your age, every single moment you sit in is bursting with potential. The door of your dreams has not been firmly shut just because time has passed.

You are always worthy of the things that your heart desires. Don't let the number that you are hold you back.

In reality, every number that we are is fleeting and none are worth getting tripped up by. What matters is that you live in acceptance of each and every moment that comes. When you can do this, the goddess in you springs into action. The inherent power of your worth starts to dance in your eyes. It becomes visible to all who look at you.

➔ power exercise for ⬅
ACCEPTING CHANGE

Preparing for the Exercise

You'll need music for this one. Find a space where you'll be comfortable with moving freely.

Doing the Exercise

Is there a change in your life that you've been resisting?

It might be something that has happened already (that you're maybe a little in denial about) or it could be something that is about to happen.

Whatever the case may be, set an intention now, in your heart, to accept this. To trust in the universe and its cycles.

After you've set your intention, it's time to clear your body out. Stand up with both feet firmly planted on the ground. Make sure your knees are slightly apart. Bend them just a drop.

Now, let your entire body go limp and shake it out. Shake out every part of yourself. Feel all of the muscles relaxing. Let your jaw hang open. Let your whole body release. If you'd like, you can turn on some music to help you keep up the momentum.

And if it's uncomfortable or not possible for you to stand, shake while seated. It's just as powerful.

After shaking out the body for ten minutes, stop moving. And feel the power present in you. Feel the flow and the willingness to accept change sparkling inside of you.

All of the obstructions, all the denials, all the refusals to accept what is—feel and know all of that is gone.

Journal about your experience afterward.

YOUR VOICE IS A POWERFUL FORCE

My husband used to run a very busy ghostwriting company here in California. For years, I worked with him, attending meetings with various clients. And in that time I noticed that there were many male clients who would pretend that I wasn't even there. The male client would talk, making eye contact only with my husband. And whenever I spoke up and added something to the conversation, he'd respond—but to my husband, as if my husband had said it.

Instead of becoming annoyed by it, it had an opposite effect on me.

These men made me feel as if I wasn't good enough. As if I didn't have anything of value to say. I let them dictate the way I felt about myself because I was unable to really see what was happening beneath the surface.

Many experiences like these made me hide my voice. They made me not want to express a single particle of what I felt burning within me. I actually started to buy into the crazy idea that my voice wasn't good enough. It was only when I started to empower my feminine nature that I realized how foolish I had been to let others drive my expression into the shadows.

Have you seen this kind of thing happen? Has it happened to you?

When a woman speaks up at a meeting or a gathering, everyone stops to listen. But they don't really hear her. She throws out brilliant ideas, she shines, radiates, but they simply don't notice.

The conversation moves on and a man starts to talk, articulating the same kinds of ideas. And everyone applauds him. Coming from a man's mouth gives it that stamp of approval.

But we must change all that.

Your Voice = Your Birthright

You have a right to speak your truth. You have a right to share your story. You have a right to be heard and respected.

Otherwise, why would you be here?

Restraining your words, limiting the gleaming truth of your natural expression, is a flow-killer. It scrambles you up inside. Your body becomes tight and heavy with all of the things that go unsaid. It carries the shadows of expressions that never got a chance to dance with form, to be heard by the ears of others.

You were not meant to restrict or constrict. To confine the potency of your own unique sound. You are here to be the fullest expression of yourself.

To do that, you must speak the truth that flickers so madly within. Rise into your power. Be a mouthpiece for wisdom, justice, and love. Let your truths intermingle with the energies of the physical plane, so that they may elevate the spirits of those around you.

Your Voice Is a Gift

Every woman's voice has a sound, a resonance, that can light the world on fire. Other people might try to interject. They might try to silence her by calling her shrill, or bossy, or a diva. They might ask her to tone it down a notch. They might demand that she throw syrupy liquids and rainbow colors over everything she's saying.

But she must keep moving forward.

The useless, idiotic chatter must not deter her.

She, *you*, must stay locked into the original, undiluted expression.

You have gold running through your veins. Pure, hot, liquid gold.

It fills up your feet and legs, grounding you, rooting you in Mother Earth. It fills the pelvis, sparking you with sensual juiciness. It moves up the body and into the heart, actualizing the force of love in you. It continues up to the throat, bringing that love energy, so fierce, to the voice that you have been gifted.

Yes. Your voice is a gift.

It's a blessing that has been bestowed upon you. And it's up to you to liberate it.

If you can feel the way your heart connects to your expression, if you can feel that gold, and those lines of energy that spread from the chest into the throat, you can give your words a thunderous quality. You can infuse them with love so mad and so deep that you will transform everybody you come into contact with.

Each word that flows out of you will be like an act of vibrant devotion. Like a missile of peace, firing into potent space. Everywhere you go, everywhere you unleash your expression, the world will vibrate anew. The colors around you will appear bolder, sharper. All that you see will be glowing. Because the world around you changes. It amps up its frequency when you are in your power. It takes on a new kind of life and energetic potency that crackles with possibility.

You have so much power in your throat.

But it is nothing if you don't use it. If you retain the wisdom of your words, nothing happens. The genius of you will remain on the other side of existence.

The same goes for when you are speaking the words, but the words are not aligned with the way you feel in your body. Speaking from a false sense of self is the same as withholding. Actually, it might be even more detrimental to your heart and spirit.

Speaking in a voice that doesn't ring true, from an expression that is unnatural, will strangle the spark that is you. It will suck up all your light and keep you feeling hollow inside. After some time, you might start to believe the words. You might start to think that they actually belong to you, are of you. But this will just be the complacency talking. It will just be you cementing the mask onto your face so deeply that it will be hard to breathe.

Your wild and divine nature is coursing through you now. It desires to be known, by you and by the rest of the world. Your body and your throat are its container, its home. But it longs to roam free across rolling mountains and oceans that overflow. It seeks form. It dreams of being felt, held, heard, and embraced so that the beauty of your infinite self can be known.

So you must show up. Express your voice. Let the words come pouring out. And don't ever be afraid to connect your heart to what you're saying. That is what's true. That is what it's all about.

Women can change this world. But not if we're meek and unexpressed. We can change this world by using our voices to speak out against oppressors, to lead a movement, to boldly go into the realm of emotions and express the things that we feel.

We desperately need women to do these things. For ourselves, and for each other. We must not use our words to disempower, to threaten, to harm or ridicule or judge. We must reach in and tap something that is deeper and greater than all that.

Once we can do that? Transcendence.

⇥ *power exercise for* ⇤
EXPRESSING YOURSELF

Preparing for the Exercise

Get ready for this soothing exercise by finding a comfortable place to sit, either on the floor or in a chair.

Doing the Exercise

This meditation will help you to feel more fully expressed in the world.

Sit up straight and close your eyes.

Focus on your throat.

Take a deep inhale through the nose, sending that breath down into the throat.

When you exhale, imagine that you are melting your throat down into the heart. So it's as if the act of exhaling is allowing the throat to dip down and merge with your heart energy.

Let's try this again.

Inhale and send the breath to the throat.

And then exhale and envision the throat melting down to fuse itself with the heart.

Do this for five minutes, and really feel your expression intermingling with the energies of love. It's almost as if your expression center is getting jump-started and sparked by the heart.

Extra Badass Tip:

After this meditation is over, take some action. Express something to someone else—something that you've been longing to say. It doesn't have to be major and overly thought out; it can be a simple sentiment of love and appreciation. The idea is that with your expression center drenched in love, you should feel empowered. Trust that your words will come from a loving and powerful place. And once you express those things that you hold in your heart, take a moment to feel the energy of your world transforming around you.

YOUR VAGINA IS ALWAYS TALKING TO YOU. ARE YOU LISTENING?

In Sanskrit, the vagina is known as the "yoni." In ancient times, it was widely revered by various cultures. The yoni was seen as the Ultimate Mother. In India today, the yoni continues to be worshipped as a life-giving, creative, all-powerful force. There are huge statues of yonis that have been created around the country. There are even temples and worship centers that are devoted to paying homage to the mysteries of the yoni.

Many people will agree—both men and women—that the whole idea and process of giving birth is nothing short of a miracle. The vagina's role in this, of course, is essential and breathtakingly astounding. There's no question about that.

The real question here: What gives with all the misogyny, then? When women demonstrate such magic and power in their bodies, when they carry endless creative prowess and potential within their physical form, why are we looking the other way? Why are we pretending that it isn't good enough?

Is it perhaps because it exceeds the idea of "good enough"? Is it because woman is so defined by her power, her fortitude, her insight, her imagination, that the world couldn't help but quiver at the mere thought of it? Intimidated, the world felt it had no choice but to tame it somehow. A culture had to be created where the obvious power on display was shielded, made to feel weaker and less than.

It's almost as if it was decided that the yoni be deemed something separate from woman. As if a woman had nothing herself to do with the actual workings of the yoni.

Woman has been separated from the body that she owns. It has been taken over. There are others out there who think it is their right to invade her yoni or to make laws that would tell her what to do with it. She has been subtracted from her most essential power source.

The Last Time I Saw a Vagina Walking Down the Street Was ... Never

Have you ever seen a vagina walking down the street all by itself? I would bet my life you haven't. A vagina can't exist without a woman attached to it. Without a woman animating it with her essence.

The world will acknowledge that the yoni performs miracles in birthing life, but at the same time, women and young girls are kept from any kind of deeper wisdom about what their vagina really means.

If you ever had any doubt about it, let's clear that up here and now.

Your vagina is overflowing with beauty and significance. It is a divine extension of your spirit, of your voice. It is your chance to know yourself and to exceed any barriers that have been placed before you. It is alive and radiating with electricity. It is a revolution of pleasure. It is a place where the frequencies of birth, love, and creation continually dance, blessing the temple that is your body.

You carry that inside of you. It isn't outside. It's there.

Which makes you nothing short of a walking miracle.

The Truth Behind the Myth

Between your legs is a jewel that, in many cases, has yet to be unearthed. And she is a beauty, in every sense of the word. Nothing can dilute her essence.

Yet still, at some point, you might find yourself succumbing to the myth that she is inherently lacking. That there is something wrong with her.

The way she bleeds every month. The way she throbs, secretes, and pulses.

You will try to tame her. To scrub her clean. To dull down her natural luster.

She will make you feel things. Sensations that seem to want to swallow you whole. Callings that feel bigger than your physical body can handle.

She will rage at you in the night. Fiercely whispering for you to wake up from your dream and accept her for all she is. You will toss and turn and your thighs will clench. You will try to convince yourself that all of this is in your head.

You will wring your hands until they are as raw as her longing.

You will go about your day, pretending she doesn't even exist. There will be no words about her to anyone. You will keep her under wraps. Private and sealed, as you have been taught.

Some days you will invite someone inside of her. And there might be times that you notice her hardening, denying access to her innermost sacred parts. Since she is laced with divine intelligence, she understands, quite deeply, who is worthy of her pleasure. She is the gatekeeper of your highest self. And so she will physically clench in the presence of a lover who doesn't deserve you. Who cannot even begin to comprehend what a marvel of a woman you truly are.

And then there will be other times. Times when you invite a lover in and you feel a kind of internal sigh. A magical state of surrender where everything opens and relaxes with a courageous "yes."

This is the receptive nature of her. This is who she is, in her truest form.

Her power lies in her ability to receive with graceful abandon. When she feels safe and honored, she will gift you with her magic. Make you feel as if your heart and your spirit have been drenched in her light.

When she is shamed, or you go too long without nurturing her, she will shut down on you. Go numb. Rendering you numb in return.

This is the power she has. Vagina, pussy, yoni, snatch, muff. Whatever it is you want to call her. Whatever name lights you up. Whatever you ascribe to her, she will be. On the surface, that is. Meanwhile, she will wait quietly, sometimes loudly, for you to know her in her truest essence.

There Is an Entire World Undulating Deep Within

She is a seeker of pleasure. A bringer of life. A creator. A mystical opening. A keeper of endless mysteries.

She is also coordinated with your deep expression. When you neglect to nourish the force that she is, when you don't love her with every aspect of your being, she will signal for your throat to close. The less orgasms and pleasure you have, the less you will be able to freely express yourself. The vagina and the throat are madly intertwined. The throat follows the vagina's lead, taking cues from her openness. Her natural lubrication sparks the lubrication of your expression center. This is why, for a woman who is seeking to be in her power, pleasure and sensuality must be embraced by the whole self.

Pay attention to this divine part of you. There is a lot to learn from her. There is an entire world undulating deep within.

If you ignore your vagina, it will be like constructing a dam inside of her walls. She will put all of her energy into holding and containing all of the pleasure so that you cannot feel it. It will not move.

The inner life will become sterile, sanitized. The outer life, in turn, will reflect this. You will feel a lack of energy, passion, and love. The waves of orgasm that would like to move so freely throughout your entire body will settle and dry up. Your fierce feminine spirit will look for ways to be expressed. But it will come up short and unfulfilled if those ways have nothing to do with loving on the vagina.

So here we go. Time for some badass power tips...

→ power tips for ←
WAKING UP THE YONI

Don't let your yoni be something separate from you.

Make a lover and a co-creator of her. Touch and awaken the pulse of life that she is.

Feel her. Listen to what she's telling you.

If shame or guilt has made a home inside of her, tell 'em to pack their bags.

Massage her into bliss.

Be conscious about who you let inside of her.

Wear sexy underwear, ones that make her feel good. Seduce her into trusting you, into knowing that you are ready for her and all the wild beauty that she brings.

Your life will break wide open as a result. You will know yourself as a powerful woman, able to create, feel, and do whatever it is that your heart truly desires.

At night, as you lie in bed, place your hands over your yoni. When you inhale, imagine you are sending that breath down into her. When you exhale, imagine that breath is sensually massaging the inside of your yoni. Continue breathing like this for ten minutes. Feel the natural vibrancy waking up inside of you.

Another thing to do: When you are out during the day, when you are walking down the street, feel the sensation of her. Feel the way she is affected by your movement. Find pleasure in this simple practice of being aware. Find pleasure inside the yoni as you walk.

And if you're a woman who doesn't have a yoni, you can still wake up this portal of energy within you. Pay attention to your pelvis/genital area, applying all of the above tips to that space. Just as powerful.

Pleasure does not need to be reserved for times of lovemaking or self-pleasuring. Pleasure is a part of you. It is a part of your vibration. It lights the spark that you are. Don't miss an opportunity to feel it bubbling up within you. Open the door to the pleasure that has been knocking so thunderously, night after night. Move with pleasure. Taste with pleasure. Drink, dance, and talk with pleasure. Your yoni will notice. She will pick up on this new energy that you are cultivating, and she will soften. She will open and flower. She will bring you back home to yourself, to where love is and always has been.

BLEED LIKE YOU MEAN IT

WHEN I WAS IN my teens and twenties, I used to despise my period. Every time it came around, I wanted to hide. It was an annoyance to me. A wrench thrown into the works. An enemy of my daily to-do list that made me think I should constantly be doing, doing, doing.

So this is how I "got out of it": I went to the gym and I worked out like a maniac. At some point, I had discovered that if I worked out hard, if I really pushed myself, I could bring my period down from five days to two days. And three less days of bleeding was like a blessing to me.

So I pushed myself. I rallied against the blood that was streaming from within me. And whenever my period ended, I felt victorious. Like I had somehow fooled it and gotten away with something. I bragged to my friends about this discovery I made and how I had found a way around it. They were all impressed and said they would try it. It seemed that the general attitude around me (and obviously within me) was one of wanting the whole period thing to be as brief and painless as possible.

At the time, I didn't realize this was me succumbing to the masculine system. It was me not realizing my own innate feminine power. From the very first drop of each and every bleed, I was already wishing it away.

I felt this most acutely after I experienced a miscarriage. At the time, my husband and I were so heartbroken. We were trying to have a second baby and the miscarriage shocked and saddened us. Where I once felt the pulse and excitement of life radiating in my womb, now there was this great big hollow nothingness that existed there. I remember clutching my belly for weeks after, hoping to detect a sign of life. Hoping that maybe, somehow, there had been a mistake.

In the months that followed the miscarriage, I tried to get pregnant again. But each month, my period came, its bright, screaming redness a reminder of yet another failed attempt. Somehow, another loss. I resented menstruation so deeply at the time. Ironic, because that whole process is necessary to sustain and support the act of creation.

But I wasn't thinking about that. I just wanted my baby. I just wanted to find some way to fill in the emptiness that had been left inside of me.

Several months later, I did get pregnant. My period was late by a day, and I just knew. My husband and I were beyond elated. By not seeing the red, we had triumphed.

When I started to understand the significance and power of my period, and the ways in which it was actually an opportunity—aligning me to the most raw and truthful aspects of my being—it was as if my entire universe cracked open.

Let It Flow

When you bleed, you are beyond powerful.

That is because the flow of menstruation mobilizes the flow of your being. You are in your fullness. Exceeding the scattered nature of your parts, becoming the tantalizing whole.

Your bleed puts you in the center of your authenticity. It summons up all of the force inside of you, liberating the seed of your essence. As your blood flows, you bloom. The mysteries of the feminine move and breathe inside your body. Nature, the moon, the cosmos. All is articulated in you, through you, from you.

Your every action, your every nonaction—all of it in service to the deepening of the mystery.

Menstruation is a sacred act, and if you surrender to the process of it, you will know the mesmeric power of all that you are. You will feel yourself from the inside. The life that dwells in your heart will make a blatant display of itself. It will leak out through your eyes like moonbeams. It will intoxicate you to the point of unapologetic expression. You will become everything that you ever dreamed you could be.

This is possible. It doesn't have to be some far-fetched fantasy, dangling in the sky, out of reach. It can be your reality right now.

It's as simple as honoring your bleed. Cherishing every droplet that flows from your body. Waking up to the natural wonder that you truly, and so very deeply, are.

To honor your bleed, you've got to do away with making an enemy of what so many refer to as "that time of the month."

Surrender.

Give yourself over to the natural cycles of your body. If women stopped looking at their period as if it were an inconvenience and instead an opportunity to realign themselves to their power, imagine how thrillingly delightful this world would become.

Imagine millions of women and girls around the world falling in love with their bodies and, in turn, themselves, and, in turn, everything and everyone around them. That'd be some bold transformation right there. The kind that shifts tectonic plates around and does some pretty harsh damage to the parts of our culture that refuse to celebrate what woman is.

Do you feel a great big *yes* inside of you right now?

If you do, that means you are feeling the pull of something greater than yourself. That means it's time to cozy up to your power.

All of us. Women everywhere. We must stop fighting against our bodies so that we can start to crack open the shell that has kept us hidden.

Your Period Deserves a Party

Right now, take a moment and breathe. Feel the delicate majesty of everything that is you. Feel the life that courses through you. Feel your inherent worth and the way it warms the body. This is always there inside of you. This is who you are. *This is why you bleed.*

So let's try this.

What if, instead of sighing when the blood started to flow, we actually celebrated it?

What if we allowed ourselves to feel the excitement of menstruation?

What if, instead of focusing so hard on the bloody mess that's being created, we focused on the power of what that blood symbolizes? Birth. Creation. Cosmos. Nature. Mother. Love. Do you have any idea how deliriously epic all that is? All of that is what you are. What you contain within your vibrant feminine being. You are a goddess, a queen, and an angel, all rolled into one. You are the answer to every question that has ever been and will ever be asked.

Do you see how powerful that is?

The things you could create, if you fully understood this power. The things you could transform.

When you're in your power, not only is your life way better, but so are the lives of everyone else around you. When you instead deny the marvel that is your body, that is your nature, you deny your own right to be here. You deny your right to live fully and deeply. You disfigure the truth of your soul.

Cutting off your own light impacts you and every single person that you come into contact with. When your light gets dulled, so do many other lights in the process.

Why This Goes Deeper Than Wearing White Pants

I spent way too many years fighting against my bleed. Trying to end it early or press on in spite of it. Resenting the fact that I couldn't wear white pants or be free to pursue my usual activities without adjusting.

But this goes deeper than white pants.

Your period isn't keeping you from doing or being anything. It's actually enhancing what you are.

Let's look at day one of your cycle to understand what's happening here. Day one represents the day that your bleed starts. When you're bleeding, your body is releasing the egg that didn't get fertilized during the last cycle. But that's not all that's happening. You're not only releasing this egg…you're also shedding away the energies of the last cycle as well.

Menstruation is about surrender and release. It's a clearing away of the past so that the new cycle can begin. With this clearing away of the past, all of your stuck emotions, disappointments, fears, and blockages are released as well. The bleed is your time to let go, so that you can start fresh. Release any and all energy that is in the way, that might hinder or inhibit you during your next cycle.

This is why bleeding with conscious awareness is important. It isn't enough to be okay with the fact that you're bleeding, and to even love the act of it. Those aspects are important too, but you must also be aware and awake to the process.

As the blood flows, feel the release. Feel the ways in which your body relaxes and makes space for the new. Feel the power that is gushing through you and from you.

This is heavy work. Although I'm saying that we must love this process, we must also acknowledge the deep work that we're taking on. This is not minor. This can't be chalked up to business as usual. Every cycle will have a personality all its own; if you start to become conscious about how you bleed, you will start to discover this. During those cycles when you've experienced the most difficulty, maybe some pain and heartbreak, you will notice that your bleed is much heavier. During times when there is less upheaval, the flow will be gentle and full of ease.

The body is beyond wise. The mind tends to protect us by stuffing away any uncomfortable feelings, but the body will never lie. It will always hold on to any discomfort that has not been dealt with and processed. It will hold on to these things and wait for a time like menstruation, when it can start to clear some of these things out.

Being more conscious about menstruation will help us to be actively and mindfully involved in this transformational process. And when we're involved, that's when the real magic happens. That's when we can understand more deeply who we are, how we hold on to things, and how we can start to release them.

⇥ power exercise for ⇤
MENSTRUATING CONSCIOUSLY

Preparing for the Exercise

As your body is doing this work of releasing, set aside some time to nurture yourself and slow down so that you can fully be aware of the beauty of what's transpiring within you. A day before your period starts, set up your own cozy space, draped in red fabric, where you can rest, meditate, journal, and reflect.

Doing the Exercise

During your period, you are most deeply aligned with your power, but this doesn't mean you need to be pushing yourself to your breaking point and powering through your day.

On the first day of your period, really make a point to stay aware and in a state of natural ease to allow the blood to flow freely.

Sit in the special spot that you've created and just let yourself be. Don't try to do anything. Just surrender to the flow. Self-care is key here, so reflect, give yourself a shoulder rub, do breathing exercises, daydream…do whatever it is that the queen in you requires. Take as long as you are able to for this exercise. Feel into your power as a woman, and know that the blood that flows from you is sacred.

While you're bleeding, while you're in that place of power, in that place of flow and creation, you will feel what it is you are gravitating toward in life.

If there is an action you must take, a conversation you need to have, a plan you must begin to explore, then move in that direction. Never force it, but flow toward it and with it. If, instead, you feel you must continue resting and nurturing yourself, don't be shy in engaging in self-care. This is the time when you need it. Listen to your body and cherish it for the work that it is constantly doing to keep you in motion.

Lisa Lister, author/creator/badass of all things menstruation, likes to take the entire day off on the first day of her cycle. She spends the day slowing down and honoring her flow, and I absolutely love that about her. (If you don't know about this woman, you've got to look her up. She's an expert on menstruation and has written books solely devoted to that topic.)

I like to take the time to nurture myself on the first two days of my period, and I also like to create and plan. When I'm beginning my cycle, I feel more and more powerful with every bit of blood that is released, and I notice that my abilities to write and envision are sharpened. I take advantage of this by writing and setting aside some time to lay out my plans for the next cycle.

Whatever you do, take the time to slow down and do something, anything, that makes you feel good. Drink some hot tea, read pages from an inspiring book, give your neck a little rub. Tending to yourself will only deepen your connection to your bleed.

After slowing down and practicing some self-care, you'll be ready. You'll be able to consciously step into the beginnings of this new cycle with clarity, purpose, and peace. It's like clearing the pathway of all the rocks, the tangled twigs and leaves, so that you can saunter across it, toward all of your hopes and dreams.

If you can become conscious of this, you will be amazed to discover all the ways in which your cycle affects you; then you'll find that it becomes quite natural to live with more focus and joy.

Working with the Moon

If you weren't born with a uterus or you don't menstruate, you can still align to the power of menstruation by using the moon to stay in tune to your natural feminine cycles.

The relationship between moon and woman is unlike any other. Just like woman, the moon goes through a twenty-eight-day cycle, waxing and waning, growing from a new moon to a full moon, and then back to new moon again. At the new moon, it's time to empty ourselves of what we no longer need so that we can start building anew. When the moon is full, the energy within you will be more vividly expressed. This is the time of deep creativity, movement, and action.

Regardless of whether or not you menstruate, it's very helpful to track the phases of the moon. As the moon grows bigger and expands its energy, you will feel the energy of your own body and mind expanding as well.

Some women menstruate on or around the new moon and others menstruate on or around the full moon. Wherever you fall is just right for you. And again: if you don't menstruate, you can still connect to this power. I created this exercise just for you.

→ *power exercise for* ←
WOMEN WHO DON'T MENSTRUATE

Preparing for the Exercise

Sit outside under the dark sky, under the moon.

(If this isn't possible for whatever reason, you can stay indoors.)

Doing the Exercise

Close your eyes. As you take a deep inhale through the nose, imagine you are pulling the energy of the moon in through your nostrils. Breathe it into your entire body. When you exhale, feel that energy of the moon dispersing throughout your entire body, like waves and bursts, vibrating across your inner space.

Continue to do this. Inhale the energy of the moon through your nostrils and into your body; exhale and disperse that energy through the body.

Notice how this makes you feel, without judging or trying to control it.

Try to do this for a good ten minutes. And trust that whatever you feel, whatever result you get, is absolutely perfect for you.

Extra Badass Tip:

Do this each night, and see if you can notice the differences between the energy, as the moon is constantly changing and offering up various expressions. Also, be sure to take the opportunity to do this on a new moon and a full moon.

→ power exercise for ← WOMEN IN MENOPAUSE

To women who are in menopause: you are just as powerful as ever, if not more so. This is a juicy time in your life, one of ultimate wisdom and evolution. By passing into the stage of menopause, you are stepping into the power of the wise woman crone, who deeply embodies the potency of birth, life, death, and cycles. Some women might feel a sense of loss when their period goes away; that's normal with any big change or transition, especially when it comes to our bodies. But as you begin to settle into yourself and feel into the ways in which you've grown and evolved into this truth-bearing, wisdom-wielding, shamanistic goddess, you'll start to find your ground again. Here's an exercise to align you to your power.

Preparing for the Exercise

For this exercise, you'll need a shawl to wrap around your shoulders. Once you're ready, find a comfortable, quiet spot to sit in.

Doing the Exercise

Place the left hand on your heart and the right hand over your womb and pelvis. Breathe for a moment here. In your mind, as you inhale, draw a strong line of energy from the heart down to the womb. And as you exhale, retrace that line of energy from womb to heart. Continue this way, retracing the line down on the inhale, and retracing up on the exhale.

Feel the energies of love and compassion blessing your womb, your pelvis, your yoni, reminding you of the power inherent in your body and in your ability to flow through each cycle.

If you feel any resistance with this, slow down. Be gentle with the way you approach this exercise and allow yourself to softly fall into a rhythm with this one.

Extra Badass Tip:

Bless your shawl by placing your hands over it, and imagine the energy from your heart coming through the arms, out the hands, and into the fabric. Wear your shawl on special occasions or whenever you want to be reminded of the power you carry.

TAKING SEX BEYOND THE BEDROOM

—

I USED TO THINK that my sexual life and the rest of my life had to be separate. I used to believe that the entirety of my sexuality was supposed to be confined to the space of the bedroom. But this isn't so. Far from it.

First off: in order to create you, a million forces had to be summoned.

Wild and delicate energies met in unfamiliar places, conspiring to fuse and merge. Thousand-year-old thought forms crumbled. Fragments of light bent themselves in exotic, unknown directions.

And then, to clinch the deal, another kind of energy had to occur: the energy of sex. The act of lovemaking. Without that, the plug of your form would've had no socket to slide itself into. You simply would not be, in a physical sense. Even if all of the other elements had come together, doing their job to create you, you still wouldn't be here, as you are, without sex.

Sex is an undeniable force.

It is creative power at its fullest. It is a sacred and all-consuming energy that pulses fiercely within. Sometimes we can feel it penetrating our every cell. Sometimes it seems to vacate the body entirely, and we become lost, dull-eyed. That is because being disconnected from our sexual energy is like having our access to oxygen ripped away.

Sex energy is life force energy. It is Shakti. When we, as women, can firmly sit in the center of it, without fear, our power will become known to us.

But we've spent way too much time shying away from the sexual power and juiciness that we feel within. Lots of this is due to the nonstop objectification of women, and also the fact that sex has been stripped of the sacred in this culture that we've constructed. Sex has been made into some cheap product to be easily consumed and gulped down. A way to get off before going about one's business. Between some people, it turns into a mechanical act; one that involves no expression of the deeper layers, of the love that is wrapped away so tightly within.

In many ways, we don't dare tread into the waters of our sexual fullness, because it's a gigantic task. To claim your power as a sexual being, without limitation, without worry of what that might look like to the other people around you—that's a scary thing.

What would that even look like?

Sex Must Exist Beyond Your Bedroom

The old must die to open up space for the new. This means shattering the mental culture that designates woman to her "proper place," where she must look, speak, think, and feel in accordance to principles that exist miles outside of her.

It means taking a breath and braving it. Revealing the sexual spark that you are. Oozing sex energy from your every particle.

Now, by "oozing sex energy," you're not sauntering in the streets, offering yourself up physically to anyone who would look your way. That's society's superficial definition of what "oozing sex" looks like. This definition that we're playing with is not even in the same universe. This definition is deeper, more divine. It is shot through with unrestricted truth. It is a sacred understanding of the greater power that binds us all, and a willingness to express—or at least attempt to express—the depth of that understanding.

Oozing sex, in the universe of feminine power, means that you're not holding back.

It means that you are in deep possession of your senses and madly in love with your body.

It means that you make no apologies for the strong vibration of emotion and passion pouring from you.

It means that the circuitry within the temple of your feminine body has been recognized as holy and that you have made the decision, here and now, to shower it with all of your courageous attention.

So that the tingle you feel while you're out grocery shopping—the one in your yoni, breast, thigh, neck, or wherever—need not be ignored and pushed back into the darkness for some later time.

Because that tingle is aliveness.

The sensations of pleasure, of orgasmic bliss, of being turned on, of being hot and bothered—that is your sexual self longing to be expressed through every waking moment. That energy is simply called being alive. Take it out of the bedroom. Stop delegating your pleasure to your partner. That pleasure is there for you to know and move with, during every second of your every day.

Some of us, if we don't have a partner or if we're not sexually active with our partner for whatever reason, get frustrated. We shut down our sexual side and think we have no outlet for the energy.

But we do. That outlet is called life.

Sexual energy—the energy that created you, the energy that flows through and charges everything the eye can (and can't) see—is there, waiting to be owned by you. To be taken beyond the shadows and the backrooms. To be lifted up from the seat of shame and guilt that it has been placed upon.

Nobody can do this work of reclaiming that power except for us. We can shake our heads, we can lament about the state of sex, about the ways in which women aren't being received and loved and touched how they should be, but that doesn't do anything for anybody. It doesn't help women or men. It doesn't deepen the conversation or impact the flow of energy in a meaningful way.

You've got to move that energy on your own.

With this body, this heart, this spirit that you have right now. In this time and place.

We must liberate the sexual nature that is our natural vitality so that we can step up and be the powerful light-bearers and change-weavers that we know, in our hearts, we are. By embracing our sexuality in a way that is sacred and meaningful, we step into our truth. We fearlessly become our authentic selves.

So what I'm saying to you is this: you've got to find pleasure *now*. In every breath and every movement.

With every turn of the head, there should be a natural sensation of pleasure. With every stroke of your nail against the skin—more pleasure. With every touch of air that comes through the nostrils or the lips—pleasure. With every stretch of the neck or of the back—the doors of pleasure, infinite, expanding.

If you don't experience that on a daily basis, it means you've got to start tapping that energy. You've got to start being comfortable with your body and expanding your awareness into every sensation and feeling that moves through you. Pay attention to what's happening in there. Don't let your body rage or wither in despair, without you paying attention to what's there. Get the information. It's in you. You just have to pay attention and access it. If there is discomfort or pain, you have to be aware of it first, before you can move it and create more space for your sexuality to expand into its fullness.

If you have struggled with your sexual energy because someone along the way tainted it for you ...

If your skin creeps or your heart feels heavy whenever you are reminded of any form of sexual abuse or shaming that you've endured, I want you to take a deep breath.

And when you take that breath, it will naturally sweep through your body, touching the parts of you that have been broken.

Keep breathing deeply.

And as you do so, just let yourself *feel*.

Let your breath soothe the hurt, the rage, the trauma that you stuffed away.

Keep doing this. And don't rush it; just give yourself over to this moment.

Finally, allow your breath to integrate the strong parts of you to the hurt parts of you. Feel it gathering your strength into the tender, achy, lost, and fearful parts of you. Let the strength infuse these parts with a forceful kind of love.

As you do this, know that your body is beautiful. And that you are a powerful woman. Nothing that has happened in the past can take that away from you. Your mind and body might have amassed a collection of painful imprints, the dust from the memories of what occurred. But know that those things are not you and they do not in any way change the sacredness of what you are. You are divine. You are whole and complete. And no past event, no trauma, no abuse, can alter that.

Keep breathing through this pain, on a daily basis if you can. Keep showing up for it so that you can cradle it in your arms.

It is aching for your acknowledgment and attention. It needs your heart and your breath and your wild woman strength to serve as a soothing balm.

And if you're not ready to do this exercise—or maybe you are but you find this simply isn't enough to heal the terrible trauma that you endured in your past—know that it's okay. Know that I am wrapping you in love and bowing down to all the strength that you possess. Know that where you are in your journey is where you're meant to be and that the light will find you again, my sister. It always does.

The Path Is Cleared and Ready for You

Are you ready to tear down the perfectly constructed illusion?

Are you ready to make bright red slashes across the voices and the mindsets that have been keeping your essence in the dark for so long?

If you're reading these words, I know that you are. I know that within you there has been that flicker. Those moments, here and there, of self-realization. Those times when the blazing truth of your feminine heart has made the hairs on your arms stand all the way up. Those days when your head felt a rushing clarity and you knew the power of your being.

And maybe there were also those times when you danced by the ocean, or you threw all of the old pages from your journal into the fire. Those times when you sat by the moon, pulled by some invisible force, and promised—a thousand times in one breath—to finally heal, to finally break through, to finally illuminate the spellbinding gifts that you so fearlessly carry inside of you.

You threatened the sky and the space—all that space—around you. Daring nature. Daring the world.

Raging with emotion, promising that the old habits would be abandoned. That you would finally come home to who you really are. Without all the extra padding and the quarter-truths.

And maybe that lasted for some time. You might've made good on your promise for a few days or weeks or months. But then you caught the haze in your eyes again. You disassociated from your body, from the wildfire that you naturally possess. You started hiding the spark again. The thing that animates and informs your essence.

You went back to the road that has been trampled by countless ancient footprints. You made space for the truths that weren't your own. The very truths that, in years prior, made you stream tears and bleed inauthentic expressions everywhere you went.

You forgot what you were. You forgot what it took to get you here. And that the energy of what it took to get you here was sacred, and that you carry that sacred power in you always.

That is why I wrote this book.

So that you remember.

So that you become so entranced by the memory that it gets its hooks in you and never lets go. And even if it does loosen its grip for a bit here and there, you have these words to come back to. You have a way of lovingly nudging yourself back onto the path that is wholly and uniquely yours.

You can brave the terrain of that path. Full force. You just have to trust in the power of your sexuality. Know that it is a sacred force within and that no one has any right to dictate how it should be expressed except for you.

From there, your Shakti will open for you, like the petals of a rosebud under the warmth of the sun. You will feel the temperature, the flow of your energy shifting to levels that you had no idea existed on this realm.

Be a woman, all charged up with sexual life force.

Be turned on in a way that exceeds the shallow definition of sex that has been widely accepted all over the world.

It doesn't matter how old you are. All of us are naturally meant to be lit up by this energy.

Sex should not be limited to the yoni or boxed away in the bedroom. It was meant to be used fully, during all hours of the day. This is the trick. Sexual energy is what Shakti uses to flow into the fullness of her power. Allow her that gift.

The force that created you cannot just remain in the background. It must be front and center in all that you do. Then everything in your life penetrates you deeply, becomes orgasmic.

To get to this place, you must expand your definition of sex so that your body can open itself up to the sacred power that it contains.

Here's an exercise to do just that.

→ power exercise for ← EXPANDING THE MEANING OF SEX

Preparing for the Exercise

Choose a whole day in which to integrate this exercise.

Doing the Exercise.

There is an instinct, a desire, to merge and become one with all that is around us. This is naturally there, driving the deeper story of our purpose here on earth. That merging, that oneness—that is sexual energy. That is sex. That need to connect so intimately and openly. In doing so, pleasure ensues.

For this exercise, I want you to take the day to create this feeling of sexual energy in the ordinary things that you encounter. That feeling of merging and becoming one with something else—find it in all of your conversations and actions.

Be so wildly present that it's almost like you are merging with that thing or that person that you are coming into contact with.

For example, if you're talking to somebody, focus only on that person. Breathe deeply so that you stay rooted and connected to your own body, as you devote every drop of your attention to this being before you. Give them your full presence. Grant them access into you.

This should feel really good. You might notice a certain sensation, an energy shift, or a tingle. That's the spark. That's the sexual energy that I'm talking about.

You can even do this when you're outdoors walking through nature. Feel the trees, the ground, the sky, as a part of you. Merge so completely with all the elements around you that a kind of pleasure tickles you from within.

Continue to build and notice this energy happening in you throughout the entire day. Merge and become one with all that you are experiencing and you will become acquainted with that sexual power.

badass self-care for
THE BODY

Your physical form endures so much, day in and day out.

We are in a constant, never-ending dance that requires a great deal of our energy, emotions, attention, and love. All of these things, whether they are negative or positive, make impressions on the body. And the body must be consistently balanced and cared for so that you can be more fully in your power.

Without self-care for the body, you lose connection to your spark. The flame dies out. It cannot sustain. It cannot keep pummeling forward without an outlet, without a way to restore and recharge. Our sacred containers hold so much light and power. Let's honor them by caring for them, by staying in deep communion with them throughout each day, so that we never lose that understanding of ourselves.

Now, here's the thing: You won't find me telling you to schedule your monthly (or weekly, or daily) massage or to book yourself a good Reiki session. You know exactly what you need in that regard.

Since I'm more focused on badass self-care, the kind that is of a sustainable focus, I'll be sharing something a little different here.

⇒ badass self-care ritual for ⇐
THE BODY

Preparing for the Exercise

Your body is always speaking to you. Do you hear it? Do you hear the things that it so desperately wants you to know? The things that will bring you back to a space of fulfillment and balance?

This exercise will help you pave the path toward this.

Turn on some sensual music. Make sure it isn't too upbeat.

Lie down on your back.

Doing the Exercise

Start to breathe into your belly. Feel the music flowing through you.

Begin to stretch your body in all directions, in every way possible. Let all your movements flow into each other.

Allow yourself to be guided by the body. Feel the ways your body wants to stretch.

Don't merely listen to the mind telling you what your next move should be. There's a huge difference between what the body wants and what the mind wants.

I say that in all matters of the body, the mind should absolutely be excluded. Feel your way through this exercise. Move for your body. From your body. Your body carries such deep wisdom. It is wildly aware of how it needs to move, which emotions are stuck in which areas, and which inner energies are yearning for expression.

Let this guide you. Because if you do, it will heal and invigorate you.

After you do this, try to sprinkle this wisdom into your daily life. Become more aware of your body. Listen to what it needs. Stop what you're doing once in a while so that you can check in to that deeper wisdom that shines in you like a jewel. If you feel you need to stretch or shake something out or circulate your hips, liberate that expression.

Jump in and start self-caring for your body daily, as needed, and this will align you to your vibrancy and power.

SECTION III
→ HEART ←

LOVE SO HARD YOU
FIND YOUR PURPOSE

I KNOW A WOMAN who feeds a string of neighborhood cats. At least fifteen of them. Some are strays. You can tell which ones just by looking at them. Their fur is coarse and scraggly, their bodies eerily thin. Most of them have homes, yet still they come to this woman's house every morning, looking for food and companionship. Looking for a warm place to sleep under the many colorful and fragrant rose bushes that line the woman's front yard.

She spends $200 a month on food. Comes out twice a day to leave gigantic bowls of dry and wet meals, along with water.

This ritual is time-consuming and financially draining, yet every single day this woman shows up to take care of these cats and allows them to lounge all day in her garden. She does this for one reason alone.

Love.

She and her husband love the cats, and so this routine goes on. Out of love.

Love has no concern with convenience. It is fueled by something greater. It is the invisible pulse that vibrates within, connecting us to all that is. And it is the power source, in every woman, that has the potential to uplift and change the world on a massive scale.

Love is the motor that keeps a goddess like you in motion. It is the lifeblood of your creative and dynamic expression. It never makes demands of you. All you are required to do is to keep your heart open to it, to use your being as a funnel for it, so that its energy can spill out into the world around you.

Love should not be kept locked away in a compartment. It should not be reserved for a single person. It should not be kept hidden when you're in the office or in your car. This jams the energy. Love cannot flow properly when it is only channeled toward specific people and areas of your life. It needs the room and space to move freely in all directions.

To accomplish this, you must vibrate love. You must be love itself, fully and completely. You must love all, even those who confuse and frustrate you. You must love the fear and the frustration as much as you love the joyful moments.

You must breathe love. When you wake up in the morning, rise with love. Stretch with love. Greet the sun with love. Make breakfast with love. Pull close the ones around you with love.

Become so immersed in the being of it that you forget your own name.

➔ *power tips for* ⬅
UNCOVERING YOUR PURPOSE

Let the words "love it or leave it" be your mantra. You can use this mantra to uncover your purpose.

Many of us go through our days unsure of exactly what we should be doing. How we should serve. What gifts and talents we should be sharing with the world.

But love answers these questions for you. Love never lies.

If you feel love spreading through your body like wildfire every time you show up at a shelter to feed the homeless, that's the answer. It doesn't need to be complicated. Locking into your purpose shouldn't have to involve charts, graphs, and endless discussions. Just tune in. If every cell in your body isn't vibrating with the word *yes* while you're engaged in something, look into that. That's probably not where your purpose lies.

Your purpose lies in the things that make you lose all sense of time and space. These are the things—the experiences, the creative flourishes, the sacred moments—that have their grip on you so totally that the hours feel like minutes. You don't mind pouring your sweat and energy into these things because these things tap the soul. They wake up something inside of you. They remind you that there are always stars twinkling amidst the dark spaces.

Your purpose can be anything. It doesn't have to be a job. Your purpose can be making others laugh. It can be baking. It can be biking, giving hugs, picking up trash in public places, juggling bananas, writing children's books, fighting against injustice, or blogging about music.

Just follow the love, and it will lead you, just as it leads the woman who rises each morning to feed cats.

When everything you do is inspired by love, you naturally stop making space for the things that don't matter. Love magnetizes your being, moving you toward all that is in alignment with your truth. You stop putting time and energy into the places and people that you are not meant to be involved with. And yes, you can still vibrate love and choose not to give your energy away to certain people.

Being love does not mean that you are without physical boundaries. Being love does not mean that you're required to allow other people to drain you. When you vibrate love, you must first and foremost have respect for yourself. That is the ultimate love. That is the beginning from which all possibility springs.

SELF-LOVE IS WHAT WILL SET YOU FREE

THERE IS SO MUCH to love about you.

Even when your hair's all tangled or you say the thing you shouldn't have said, there's a beauty in you. An unrefined kind of poetry that exudes tremendous grace.

You are a gold mine of endless wisdom, power, and peace. There is nothing beyond your reach. You are a creatress who glides between worlds, unifying all that is, blessing the earth beneath you just by walking upon it.

There is nothing you can't do. There is no wall you cannot climb, no ocean too rough for you to swim across.

It might not feel like that a lot of the time.

A lot of the time it might feel as if you are stuck. Like there's a heavy barrel in your hands that you're being forced to carry. Your fingernails are digging into this barrel and you're feeling the burn. But for the life of you, you can't let go. You just can't. Not yet. You know you should, but...

There is too much to unravel, too much to process and reflect upon. Maybe you feel you haven't shed enough tears yet—or maybe you haven't shed any at all. And so you're just holding on for when the time's convenient. You're holding on to this collection of hurts and fears that you have amassed over the years. And you cannot love yourself—you simply cannot—as long as this barrel is a part of the picture.

Does this sound about accurate? Are you putting off loving yourself because of the things you have not yet released?

Things like:

> The negative self-talk.
> The disempowering beliefs.
> The past.
> The insecurities.
> The failures.
> The times your heart got broken.
> The nonstop self-judgments.
> The body hate.
> The times your dreams got stomped on.
> The things your friend said.
> The things your lover said.
> The things your parents said.
> The depression.
> The anxiety.
> The feelings that make you feel as if you are
> living every hurt you've ever experienced, with
> stunning precision, all over again.

Whether you've experienced one or all things on that list, it doesn't matter. You can still love who you are.

Does that make sense?

It might seem impossible. You've got this collection, this barrel that you're carrying around with you all over the place, and it might not seem like loving yourself is the appropriate thing to do. It might seem like the appropriate thing to do, in fact, is to continue lugging that barrel around until your arms get so tired that you have no choice but to do the work of processing all the things that have hurt you. And then, maybe after you've healed and dealt with all those things, you can love who you are.

That might sound like a reasonable plan, but in actuality it's not!

There's no time to put off loving yourself. This life is short. The only thing you can be truly sure of is this moment, right now; this breath you are breathing right now. Beyond that, who knows?

So why wait? Why wait until after all the self-help books are read? Why wait until you've attended all of the classes and followed all of the best gurus around the world?

You could waste years. Decades of your precious life. You could pour countless hours into healing yourself, into cycling through all of the same negative patterns that have kept you frozen, and you might never get there.

You must love yourself now. Don't lock yourself up in a room, dutifully sanding away at your rough edges, trying to make yourself into a perfect projection of what you think you need to be, look, feel, think, and act like.

That never works. The self-love must be there first. The self-love must be the spark—the match that starts the fire.

But how do you do this, when your life has been fed with the energy of systems that have disempowered women for so long? How do you do this, when you pick yourself apart constantly? How do you do this, when you often find yourself turning over in your mind all the ways in which you are unworthy? How do you do this, when you internally sigh every time your eyes catch the mirror? How do you do this, when you so easily accept the judgments and criticisms of others, as if they have authority over you? As if the things they say are not a reflection of the way they feel about themselves?

Well, the first step is to set the barrel down.

Now, this might seem like basic hackneyed advice, but there's a profound ferocity in this simple act.

By setting the barrel down, you take the power back.

You say: I will not let my hurts, my pains, and my heartaches destroy me.

You show the barrel who's boss. You show the barrel that you will not be shut down by dead weight. The barrel will still be there. Just because you are not holding on to it, it will not disappear into thin air.

All of your hurts, pains, and heartaches have molded you. They have left their markings on your essence, on your spirit. These markings, these experiences, are part of your growth in this life. They are reminders of your strength. They are the lessons that you have learned in this life. Some of them might have stung you so viciously that you felt you might never get out of bed again, but you're still here, aren't you?

And if that's not a reason to love all of the wonder that you are, then I don't know what is.

Self-love is acceptance of everything you are in this moment. It takes bravery, which I know you have. It's the courageous act of a woman who welcomes in the dark with the same passion that she welcomes in the light.

You are both sides of the coin. You are sun and moon. You are a gorgeous medley of elements that merge in harmony amidst the energies of chaos.

That is what you are.

And that is worth loving now.

Not tomorrow. Not next week or next year.

But now.

➔ *power tips for* ➔
SELF-LOVE

Love yourself now.

You are exactly who you need to be and you are exactly where you need to be. Let this moment cradle you in the warmth of that knowledge.

Love yourself now.

Wrap your arms around your body in a great big hug and breathe as you feel into your own unique brilliance.

Love yourself now.

Walk outdoors with your head up, throat and heart open to the sky, and feel confidence shining through your beautiful being.

Love yourself now.

Close your eyes and forgive yourself for all the mistakes you've made. And vow to always forgive yourself no matter what.

Love yourself now.

Practice the art of fierce presence when you're with the ones you love. Devote your attention and energy to them as if there is nothing else that matters, and in doing so you will more deeply open up your heart.

Love yourself now.

Honor your boundaries and distance yourself from anyone who attempts to trample upon your spirit.

Love yourself now.

Be expansive in your energies and expressions and never allow self-love to distort into self-centeredness. As you love who you are, also feel into the knowledge that every other being on this planet is worthy of deep love as well.

Love yourself now. Love yourself now. Love yourself now.

Be like the stars in the sky and light the dark up with that love.

→ affirmation for ←
EMBODYING SELF-LOVE

My every thought is an expression of love.
My every word is an expression of love.
My every action is an expression of love.
I see every experience as an opportunity
To shine love outward,
Like a light
That never fades.
I am love.

INSIDE EVERY WOMAN IS A BADASS MOTHER

IN 2011, I WAS thrust into motherhood with the birth of my first son.

In the days that followed his arrival, I remember stopping every now and then to ask myself, *Am I really doing this?*

I was astounded by my endurance and devotion; by the limitless well of love that somehow propelled me toward pouring every ounce of my energy, time, and attention into this tiny new creature.

I didn't know all this was in me before. But it was there. It wasn't something that needed to be rehearsed or studied for a thousand hours. For the innate ability to mother, to plug into love and to use that love as a life-changing force in the world, is in every single woman that exists.

Regardless of whether or not you have kids, an internal mother exists within you, her arms open wide and ready to spread love.

The love of a mother does not move in dribs and drabs. It's an unrestricted kind of love. Open, airy, fortifying. Its powers are restorative. Everything it touches is blessed a million times over.

This is a love that's got the frequency turned up to the maximum volume. It's like an overflowing cup. The love starts out aiming to fill and pour itself in one direction, but in doing so it can't help but spill out into every direction. That's because its frequency cannot be contained. No net or cup or wall can keep it from realizing its natural expression.

Every woman has this. The raw, fierce, vulnerable, compassionate force that is mother. Every woman lays claim to the potency of this love. And if she can melt into this wisdom, fully take it all the way into every cell, she can liberate herself from fear or any other thing that keeps her stuck.

You don't have to have kids to know this love inside of you. This love isn't something that is just created when you become a mother to an actual child. In every mother, the love has always been there, whether she knows it or not. It has been lying dormant, waiting for the opportunity to express itself, to expand beyond what it means to be a soul living in a body that is separate from everyone else.

As women, we've got to start integrating our beings with this energy, opening ourselves up to all of the potential that exists in becoming one with the mother in us all.

If You Struggle (or Have Struggled) with Your Own Mother

Some of us might have had (and even continue to have) strained relationships with our mothers. Know that even though this might be the case for you, it does nothing to detract from your light and your ability to mother and nurture. If you struggled with your own mother growing up—if you found that she wasn't there to love and support you in the ways that you desperately needed—know that you're not alone, sister. Trust that this is not a reflection of your worth and your value.

Our society has placed endless demands upon mothers. Generations of mothers have carried a great amount of resentment, pain, confusion, sadness, and loneliness, trying to live up to impossible standards. With this burden pressing upon their hearts, some mothers have shut down, unable to keep up, unable to fully love and embrace their children through childhood and beyond.

Your mother, just as you are, is a flawed woman. She has accumulated her own pains and disappointments. If you can find ways to love, accept, and understand who she is, you can slowly start to heal your relationship with her, whether she's living or has passed on.

And if there are parts of you that you still feel have been left unloved, breathe deep into your own heart and awaken your unique nurturing energies. Allow those nurturing energies from your heart space to move through your body while you wrap your arms around yourself.

Cause mama, you've got this.

Mother Can Be Glamorous—and Sexy Too

Now, depending upon where you're at in your journey, the word *mother* might not sound glamorous or sexy to you. It might not sound hip or adventurous enough to excite you into uniting with its energy.

But let me tell you something: once you start becoming familiar with the sheer force and power of what it means to truly live from the heart of a mother, you will start to know her as a gorgeous goddess, bearing endless gifts.

Our culture would like us to look at Mother as a maternal figure who will bend over backward for her children. Who will put aside her own needs and wants to get in lockstep with those who have her heart.

Mother has become a figure who dedicates herself so deeply to the ones that she loves that any ideas of self-care or self-love get thrown out of a hundredth-story window.

Mother is doting, Mother is kind, Mother has our back, Mother loves us, no matter what.

Mother has everything under control, providing the foundation so that we can launch ourselves into the stratosphere of our own choosing.

The story of Mother and the roles we've relegated her to have actually limited her life force energy. Her Shakti—that creative, sensual, all-encompassing feminine quality—takes on a tight, masculine nature. We demand too much of her. We ask her to stretch herself in ways that aren't humanly possible. We take up space in her heart, her body, her spirit, so that she might vacate these areas.

The idea of Mother has been seized and made out to be something unlike its true self. It has become a job, a function. It has lost its deeper, more magical and endearing qualities. All this word now stirs up in the imagination is "A Woman with Kids." That's what we have sanded it down to.

The ways that the idea of "mother" has been co-opted reflect the ways that we've rolled over Mother Earth. One reveals the other. It's all the same. That energy that exists so beautifully in all of nature can be found in the heart of every woman.

As we continue to destroy ecosystems—to suck the life force out of our oceans, rivers, valleys, forests, and snowcapped mountains—as we continue to drill for oil and threaten the lives of entire species of animals, we shatter our connection to Mother Earth. She aims to expand, to be in the bloom of her fullest potential, yet we cut her short. We instead focus on pursuits of ego, of profit, of power that separates.

The whole idea, the depth of what it means to be a life-giver, a creator, a nurturer, a magical wonder—all of that gets lost in the process. The glowing, abundant, rich, and vast energies of the feminine get buried.

Blaze Forward, into the
Love-Frequency of Mother

When you step into the fullest expression of what it means to be Mother, you instantly recalibrate yourself to the frequencies of love.

These frequencies are so high, so knock-you-down powerful, that you exist in a place where you can't help but be love. So this isn't merely about showing love, expressing love, and revealing love.

It's about being love.

Fully embodying its intricate and expansive meanings, allowing your soul to know the textures of its energy, so that you can show up as love itself in everything you do.

That's where the true definition of Mother can be found. In the being of love. In the burning down of the old construct so that power can be reclaimed. So that we can rise into who we truly are as women.

When you allow yourself to become one with what Mother truly means, you wake up that powerful energy within yourself. The nurturing, nourishing, sustaining qualities that you naturally possess as a woman are lifted up to the surface, where they can move and flow. Where they can make an impact on the physical world.

Your heart starts to beat with the rhythms of Mother Nature. That connection is forged.

You breathe in her strength, and at once, know yours. You begin to feel no longer *separate from*. Your heart extends outward, toppling over all lines, all things that would like to divide.

Becoming the Mother is to know yourself without limits. It's to awaken the unstoppable force of love, light, and power that is your birthright. You have a right to know this feeling. You have a right to be the love that you've been seeking out.

No more waiting for the opportunity to awaken that love. No more looking for reasons why you must hide and protect it. No more thinking that if you don't have kids, you're not a Mother.

As woman, you are Mother.

You are the promise, the hope, of this planet.

Don't let that intimidate you into straining to figure out what action you should be taking. You don't need to do anything but be.

Exist as this love. And the rest will take care of itself.

⇢ power exercise for ⇠
STEPPING INTO YOUR INNER MOTHER
Preparing for the Exercise

Find a place that's quiet. Sit or lie down.

Doing the Exercise

To fully realize the fierce love of the Mother that you carry within, you must first start to feel that energy.

Once you feel it, you can continue to melt more deeply into it so that the feeling expands.

Start to breathe deep into your belly. Remember a time when you felt the force of love beating so powerfully within you that it felt boundless. Like there was no limit to it.

Once you've chosen the memory, allow yourself to reflect on it until you can feel something in your heart.

When you've spied a feeling in the heart, you can let go of the memory. Just focus on the feeling now. Breathe into the feeling. Let the feeling take over your attention.

If you can, try to merge the body around the heart into this feeling. Let it permeate every part of you.

Try to do this for fifteen minutes.

Once the feeling has expanded throughout your entire body, breathe and enjoy it.

Extra Badass Tip:

After the exercise, go about your day. Try to keep this feeling of love active. Do something nurturing for someone else as you feel this love circulating through you.

Try to stay conscious of this feeling that has been awakened within you.

The main thing is that your mind is tucked out of the way so that the wisdom of this love can come through and reveal itself.

If you can work to keep your mind out of your business (which is hard, I know, but you can develop this ability with some time), you can start to live more freely as love. Your body will naturally move and flow, and be the feeling of love that you carry within.

Do this exercise at the beginning of the day so that you can try to work with the energy during your interactions.

Don't get frustrated during those times when that love energy eludes you. If you find yourself caught up in a moment when that force of love seems very far away, just take a moment to tune in to your heart and say the words (either silently or out loud): "Mother. Love." Say these words, as if you are gifting them to the energy of the heart, planting their frequency there. You will feel that spark start to wake up inside of you again.

Keep working this muscle and this will eventually be effortless to you.

YOUR SOUL MATE IS OUT THERE (AND IN THERE, ALSO)

To the women still looking for love: You deserve a soul mate who cherishes your every breath. Who sees in you the beauty of a million blazing sunsets. Who makes you feel safe, warm, protected.

You deserve strong arms to pull you close. Deep eyes that look all the way into you. A voice that speaks your name as if it were the only sound.

You deserve someone who sees the luminous truth of what you are.

Someone who accepts all of your shades and intonations. Who will walk with you, intently, through every storm. Who will whisper in your ear and remind you of all the things you've forgotten.

Your heart pumps steady and strong with this knowledge. It knows that you are worthy of deep love. It has always known this. It knows this regardless of the circumstance.

The problem is that you don't always know this.

The mind processes all of your past experiences and concludes that you must not be worthy. It overrides the heart space and sinks your spirit.

But you can't let it.

The heart is one of the strongest forces that your body contains. It harnesses the vibration of love, which is the highest of vibrations. Your heart is truly a force to be reckoned with. If you allow it to lead you, it will show you your worth. It will make you feel as if that soul mate is already there.

You are a gorgeous marvel of a woman who deserves to be seen, heard, felt, and understood.

The depth of your worthiness for love is gigantic.

You must grab hold of it and live your life from that place. Move like a woman who knows that she's deserving of a soul mate who sets her heart ablaze. Instead of envisioning strong arms to hold you, make your own arms strong.

Do the work of interrupting your mind when it starts to play out the boring script that reminds you that you're not deserving of love. That will do nothing to move you forward. It will only drape your spirit in low vibration. It will block love from you.

If all of that sounds like one enormous strain, start here:

⇒ *power exercise for* ⇐
MAGNETIZING A SOUL MATE

Preparing for the Exercise

This one you can do anytime, anywhere, and in any position.

Doing the Exercise

Feel your heart beating in your chest, and to the heart, almost like a song, let these words slide off your tongue: "*I am worthy and deserving of infinite love.*"

This is what I call "heart talk." When you talk to the heart, you can revive your connection to it. You are reminding yourself of its presence and you are sparking something inside of it.

Feel each syllable of each word dropping into the heart, merging with the vibrant frequencies that are present there.

When you've finished saying the words, just settle on the heart and feel the love that throbs from within. Breathe into this feeling for a few minutes or until you feel it's naturally time to complete this exercise.

Try to do this exercise each day if you can. It'll help to align you to your worth, while cultivating a strong sense of safety inside of you. Your soul mate might not be here tomorrow, or next week, but the energy of that soul mate will be opened within you. It will give you a feeling of fulfillment, so that you are not hungering so much for love outside of yourself.

It will complete you. You will start exuding love in all directions, casting an energetic spell, calling your soul mate to you with your ethereal feminine powers—something that all women carry within yet aren't fully aware of.

FIERCE AUTHENTICITY

I KNOW HOW HARD it is to be authentic at all times.

I used to be a big pleaser who wanted all parties to be happy. I would often catch myself saying yes to things and to people that I wanted nothing to do with. And I suffered as a result of this. I poured time and energy into people whom I had no business pouring my time and energy into. I wasted hours walking down avenues that deadened my spirit.

When I became a mom is when I had the courage to stop going down this path. Now, with two little kids to love and care for, I have no time and absolutely no desire to pour energy into a life that is false. I had no choice but to start honoring myself and the things that really spoke to me. I had no idea that becoming a mom would allow me to finally start giving myself permission to just go ahead and be who I am.

This doesn't mean that you have to be a mom just to get this kind of permission. The truth is, I waited too long. I waited until I was thirty-one to get this permission. That's a whole lot of years that could've been much juicier, in my opinion. But honestly, don't wait to get that permission to start standing up for your authenticity. You don't need permission. Just decide.

This is all up to you.

You must decide to let everything just fall away—all of the posturing and the masks, all of the attachments to who you should be and what you should look like.

You must decide to trim the fat out of your life, to cut out whatever isn't in alignment with you.

You must decide to enter a place of fierce trust and love so that you can be who you are, with absolutely no apologies whatsoever.

Because when you instead reach for platitudes and polite tones, you stifle your spirit.

The life force energy of you, your feminine power—all of it takes a back seat whenever you fake a smile or say words that ring false to your heart.

A goddess relies upon the currency of authenticity to move her. Her aim is to always cultivate the raw aspects of her being, not to tame the messy parts of herself into submission. Otherwise she will become a counterfeit version of her true soul. A cardboard cutout of gestures and expressions.

But you are not that. You are so much more.

Hiding your light does nothing but detract from the sublime truth of your own unique essence.

You were not born to fake your way through. You were not destined to be merely palatable or unoriginal.

The force of your nature is demanding to be noticed by you at all times. Especially when you are throwing a wall up between what's real for you within and what you project to those around you.

When you are not true to yourself, you will feel the ramifications of that deceit showing up in your body. You will feel an ache amidst all of the fear that keeps you fixed in place.

When there is no alignment between what you feel, think, say, and do, you will always feel on edge and out of sorts. Your whole reality will suffer from a lack of center and clarity.

How many times have you said one thing to your friend, yet secretly felt differently? How many times have you felt desperate to realize your dreams, yet over and over again taken actions to sabotage yourself at every turn?

There is no alignment there. When you are saying something false to your friend, your aim is to play nice. When you are sabotaging yourself by repeating the same mistakes, you are resorting to old patterns that keep you safe and comfortable. All of those intentions are understandable...

But where is the goddess in all that?

Alignment Is Your Birthright

There is nothing more electrifying than a woman who is in full alignment. When thoughts, words, feelings, and actions come together in one great big *yes*, the vibration of this planet is amplified by the millions.

That's because this kind of woman is a woman who makes things happen. She embodies fierce trust and seems to be in a perpetual free fall of surrendering to each and every glorious moment as it comes up. There's no time for posing and playing games from this deeply aligned state. There's no time for allowing fear to throw a wrench in the works.

Because, goddess, when you're aligned, you're locked into the flow. That same flow that the hum of this very universe is centered upon. And what is this universe but a macrocosm of all those energies and potentials that ebb and flow within your gorgeous being?

Authenticity is at your fingertips. It isn't something that takes great effort. In fact, it is the opposite of effort. When you're authentic, you can stop tensing your shoulders and striving to be something you're not. Because pretending to be something you're not, continuing to keep the facade and the empty words going full force—*that* takes tremendous effort. It's the height of waste. Continuing on this hamster wheel of inauthenticity will just short you out.

And we need you. Now more than ever, we need the deeply embodied, wildly authentic goddess that is you to step up into her gifts and reveal her true power.

Authenticity Minus the Heart?
Nuh-Uh. Not Possible.

Authenticity isn't something to fear or shy away from. It doesn't require you to say rude things that will hurt other people or to blatantly push people aside to go after the things you truly want.

One of the keys to unlocking authenticity is knowing that it's a heart-based affair. I don't care who you are, you simply cannot be authentic without the heart being heavily involved in the process. The heart is the lifeblood of authenticity. It is what powers the real and the raw. It is your connection to something deeper that binds. It is love, that divine, invisible, energetic landscape upon which this entire world was created.

You can't deny this. Especially as a woman, you can't deny the power that exists in the center of your chest; the potential of what that power can do and what it can transform. If you want to honor the unique imprint of you, the heart must be the first stop.

Stop here first, then settle.

Give the heart your attention and your trust, and it will amplify. The tight rosebud will open slowly, and you will know the bloom of all that you are.

Then, when you are in alignment, when you are trying to convey the truth about what you think to a friend or anyone else, the words will not be tinged with fear. They won't stab like spears. They will instead flow with a compassion that is so stunning that the listener will feel more at ease and connected to you than they ever have been before. Your own alignment will create a vibration that will spread from you to this other person, to the entire world. And that is true power.

True power never aims to weaken, belittle, or detract. True power aims to expand, reveal, and strengthen. True power is based in love and the elevating of that love.

→ power tips for ←
CULTIVATING YOUR AUTHENTICITY

In order to make this work, you've got to start with the feelings first. Tune in and notice what you're feeling.

Because the things you think, say, and do must be dictated by that feeling. The feelings are what need to be noticed and acknowledged, first and foremost. This is something I'm going to keep reminding you about, because it is one of the most important parts when it comes to accessing your true feminine power.

You must pay attention to what you're feeling inside. Know where you are—and have the courage to fully BE where you are.

If your body has a bad feeling about a particular person, don't spend time with them anymore. If you're feeling a call within to stop by your boss's desk and have a conversation about getting promoted in the future, notice that feeling. It will help you to get things moving—to request the meeting to sit down, to refine your thoughts toward taking your goals and finessing them into reality.

Let your inner world guide you toward alignment and authenticity. It will never betray you.

Also: Your feelings are never wrong. Don't ever feel that your feelings are weak, unimportant, petty, or embarrassing.

They're not.

Your feelings, sensations, and emotions are like a collection of sacred relics that live and breathe within you.

Yes, this culture doesn't appreciate feelings as much as it should, but that does not mean you should fall for the illusion that what you're feeling isn't polished enough for prime time.

Your feelings always matter. Stay present and aware of them whenever they surface. Notice the textures. Notice how big or small each one is. Find the center of each feeling as it comes and breathe into it.

Every feeling you have is always good enough, is always worthy of your attention. Your mission now is to let each feeling be your compass and guide you on a journey toward a more electrifying path in life, one that is sparkling with so much promise.

EVERY RELATIONSHIP
IS A BLESSING

———

When I met my husband, I was eighteen—and *I just knew*.

He woke something up inside of me. Our own unique vibrations clicked together like the pieces of some cosmic puzzle. I felt the shift in me. I felt the passion and electricity that flowed between us.

At the same time, we had our differences.

He was more unafraid of speaking up and letting himself be heard. I, on the other hand, was hesitant about sharing my voice and revealing my true power.

Despite all of the love and excitement, there was a heap of discomfort.

I shrunk in embarrassment whenever he was blunt and vocal about something in front of others, and he bristled whenever he saw me holding my tongue and letting someone else walk all over me.

In the beginning, this was tough.

But I started to realize that this was what I needed. I needed him to empower that part of me that was afraid to speak my truth. I started to understand that this must've been part of some divine plan, that we called one another together, in union, to do very specific work together.

That's when I started to understand this truth: every relationship we have in life is meant to shape and evolve us.

My husband inspires and uplifts me every day, fueling me with the love that I need to keep moving forward. He also challenges me to stand in my authenticity; he sees a power in me that I sometimes lose track of, when fear clouds my vision.

And I do the same for him.

My husband is an extraordinary entrepreneur, artist, and communicator. He aims to go deep in all that he does and puts loads of pressure on himself in the process. He has a hard time relaxing and tends to clench when he knows he should be going with the flow.

With my gentle nature, I coax him back to his center. I remind him that he is much more powerful from a deep state of acceptance and a willingness to abandon all rigid expectations. This causes friction at times. There are moments when he becomes exasperated at my patience and my way of accepting people for who they are.

It's definitely a balancing act all the way around, but neither of us would have it any other way. We are here to do this transformative work together. We are here to help one another to rise into the fullness of all that we are.

Now, this story is an example of a way that discomfort can serve a purpose in stretching us.

But I just want to make clear: the takeaway isn't that a significant other is needed to grow you into who you are.

It can be a relationship with your neighbor, your coworker, or your sister. Partner or not, you have relationships, and those relationships are all here to wake you up to the core truth of what you are. I'm just using my husband as an example of a relationship that has stretched me beyond what I knew.

Another thing to keep in mind: Not every relationship you have is meant to challenge you. Some are there to simply support you, love you, provide an example that you need to see, instill awareness of a certain issue…there are a myriad of reasons. The key is to honor and cherish every relationship you have, because all of them serve a deep and sacred purpose in your life. All of them work to co-create a universe meant solely for you, so that you can have the experiences you need to flourish into the wonder of the woman that you truly are.

Every Relationship Is a Blessing

Never mistake the people in your life for random chaos. The universe worked with deep, deliberate intent to bring them to you, to bless your life with the relationships that you are currently in. All of your relationships are an outgrowth of your soul's desire for deeper expression; each and every one signifying its own unique sound, calling for you to expand more fully into your power.

The people in your life are meant to serve as your compass, guiding you down the winding path, closer and closer to your inner magnificence. This is true regardless of who the person is—a ride-or-die friend that you can't ever picture living without; an ex that stripped your sense of self-esteem from you;

a parent who completely gets you and loves everything that you are; a previous boss that questioned your every action.

Each relationship carries its own set of gifts. These gifts are ready and waiting for you to unwrap them, so that you can shift into the next phase of your journey.

Now, this might be hard to accept. There might be a chunk of resistance inside of you right now. Maybe you want to throw this book across the room, or, at the very least, throw your arms up into the air and shout, "What?!!"

Cause why should your obnoxious ex ever be considered a blessing in your life? Why even bother going there?

I'll tell you why.

Because you *can*. Because not to do so is to let fear and resentment have its way with you. It's to leave your power on the table and turn your back on acknowledging the precious frequency that upholds each and every moment.

The picture of your life is an accumulation, a medley of lights and darks, each element amplifying the next.

You could not be who you are, right now, in this very moment, without all of your relationships, without the people who both test you and awaken joy in you. These people have created possibility and movement within you. Like them or not, they have stretched you into the woman that you are today.

The woman that you are today is your launching pad.

She is the spark, the fire that will carry you, that will keep you hungry and available to transform and grow tomorrow.

The woman that you are today is worthy of being loved and accepted right now, for all that she has endured, encompassed, and expressed, up to this moment.

Every particle of your life, from the inside out, is a divine outpouring of your soul's desire for expansion.

Take a moment right now to acknowledge all of the blessings that have showed up in your life, wrapped in the form of these divine relationships.

One More Thing Before the Exercise

I understand that this might be flat-out impossible for some of you, depending upon your past and the types of people that have come in and out of your life. If you're struggling with this, just breathe and skip past the rest of this chapter for now. All of us must do this kind of work on our own time, when the body, mind, spirit, and heart are truly ready to heal and move forward. Honor where you're at and let things flow from there. It's all divine.

⤙ power exercise for ⤚
BLESSING ALL YOUR RELATIONSHIPS

Preparing for the Exercise

Make sure you have a pen and a journal or paper handy for this one.

Doing the Exercise

Make a list of all the major relationships in your life—the ones you have currently, and also the ones from the past that you might no longer have. The people on your list can be any romantic partners (current or past), parents, siblings, children, friends, and any other family members. Try to aim for anywhere between five and fifteen names.

Now write a few words next to each name that describe your current (or past) relationship with them.

After you're done with that, go back to the top of the list and write about what you've learned from each person.

Make note of the ways in which you've been strengthened by certain relationships. Write about the ways that each one has contributed to your growth. For this part of the exercise, resist the urge to write negatively about the more difficult relationships. Instead, think about the ways in which your life needed this certain person who challenged you. Trust me: you'll be surprised in the most pleasant of ways by what you discover.

Remember to breathe and stay in touch with your body as you journal. This is courageous work you're doing here.

After finishing up this exercise, you can say the words of the Relationship Blessing right here:

➤ *blessing / affirmation for* ⫸
RELATIONSHIPS

My every relationship is a blessing.
And I feel each of those blessings
Resonating in my heart.

All relationships
That have tested me
Or currently test me—
I choose to see them as sacred today.
I choose to honor and accept them,

To love the ways in which
They have taught and healed me.

All relationships
That have opened the door in my heart
That have awakened joy and laughter,
Adventure, intimacy, and comfort
Within me,
I honor them now,
For growing me,
For evolving me toward
My truest self.

I am infinitely blessed
As a result of
Every relationship,
And every person,
That has come into my life.

STOP DENYING MEN AND MASCULINE ENERGY YOUR LOVE

"Boys are so naughty."

These words from a woman walking by me on the street. She was pushing a two-year-old girl in a stroller. Meanwhile, I was standing on the sidewalk as my own two-year-old boy was crouching down and watching a worm wriggle around in a puddle of water left by last night's rain.

The woman eyed my toddler suspiciously, as if he were up to no good. Repeated the words again. This time, with emphasis. Dragging the words out.

"Boys are so naughty."

I smiled and told her that he was just being curious.

But she wasn't having it. She shook her head, brows raised, and walked off.

I think back on this silly encounter from time to time. How funny it is that a woman could imply that my toddler was naughty, simply for the fact that he stopped on the sidewalk to watch a worm on the ground. To be honest, my toddler could be considered naughty for a myriad of other reasons, but this was definitely not one of them.

The thing about the patriarchy is that it doesn't just deny women of their natural expression. It also denies men of their own expression as well. It rams the mentality of "boys will be boys" right on through. Painting the entire male gender with a wide brush, dipped in mischief, action, and brute strength. This is what infused that woman on the street with the viewpoint that all boys are up to no good, no matter what it is they're actually up to.

Men are placed in boxes just as women are. Their boxes are much different. They might have more legroom, but they're boxes nonetheless.

And the Million Dollar Question Is …

How can we ever expect for women to be equally valued and cherished, to gain the space to flower into the fullness of their own truth, when the men on this planet are also being blocked from their authentic selves?

It's simply not possible.

We cannot lift ourselves without lifting the other gender. After locating our own feminine power, and after joining forces with other women who are also standing in their worth, we must do what might initially seem impossible: we must support all men in accepting their own feminine qualities as well.

Every human being on this earth has both the feminine and masculine within them. This idea was first popularized by Carl Jung. He wrote that women are the physical embodiment of the feminine and also, internally, carry a masculine personality. At the same time, men are the physical embodiment of the masculine and carry an inner feminine personality.

Since the feminine has been suppressed and repressed for so long, and it exists in both men and women, this can only mean one thing: both genders lose. It can't be exclusive to women.

The feminine qualities of compassion, connection, empathy, and intuition can't exist for women alone to express. They must also be available for men to embrace. In fact, if men don't embrace these qualities within themselves, they run the risk of not knowing who they truly are beneath the surface. They become a half-version of themselves.

Can you imagine a more painful way of being?

Culture has driven men to scoff at revealing emotions, at nurturing others and appearing vulnerable. But these are human qualities. If we have an entire gender that is uncomfortable with revealing any kind of emotion, how can we create a better world?

Feelings and emotions are what we are. They are live currents that exist within us. In the body, the mind, the heart. If an emotion is suppressed, the entire being is suppressed. The essence will never know the vibration of freedom and expansion.

Men are not indestructible pillars of strength. They are not superhuman shields that guard against sensation. They are not cold and calculated action-takers who find all fulfillment in ego-based pursuits.

You might know some men like this, but this is just a carefully constructed illusion of themselves. This isn't who they really are. It's what fear has driven them to create and project.

Don't buy into it.

Underneath the exterior, there is a heart that beats wildly. It longs to express itself and to be fully expressed.

Don't lose sight of this fact.

When you look at a man and you have the instinct to shake your head and roll your eyes at what a buffoon he's being, stop yourself short. Instead, choose to see him with love and compassion. See beyond the fear, and know him as a sacred being, just as you are. Know him as worthy of love, joy, beauty, and peace.

Even though he might not know himself that way. Cause it's got to start somewhere.

Make the choice to be the one to take the initiative, to set the record straight. And while you're at it, claim those parts of you that the patriarchy has deemed you too weak to possess. Embrace the masculine in you. The aspects of you that take action, that thrive off of logic, that are forceful and bold.

As men have been separated from their feminine, you have also been displaced from your masculine.

Or perhaps you have been leaning too hard into the masculine your whole life, trying to be something you're not, trying to play the game and get ahead. Loosen your grip then. Stop trying to be so hard and so calculated and settle back into your feminine.

As you've been reading this book, that has naturally been happening as a result anyhow. But be conscious of the ways in which you are using your energy.

Aim, always, for balance. The more you can welcome balance into your life, the more that balance will be welcomed onto this planet.

The Patriarchy Isn't Just Antiwoman

When my dad was married to his first wife and he was raising my brother and sister, he was met with frustration everywhere he turned. That instinct of nurturing was so deeply etched within him that he had no choice but to express it. At the time, though, the world appeared unprepared for this kind of "behavior."

My dad told me a story about one time that he took my brother and sister on a bus. This was back in the sixties. They couldn't have been more than five years old at the time. He recalled getting judgmental looks from women throughout the bus that day. One even spoke up and cuttingly asked him why they weren't with their mother. She apparently didn't feel it was his job to spend the day with his kids.

Although we're leagues beyond the mindset of the women on the bus that day, men are still not granted access to their feminine. And if we want real change to happen, we must create it within ourselves. We must accept men and see them for who they truly are. We must look beyond the surface, the exterior, and see what's really there.

What's more, we must practice raw and unconditional love for all men.

Now, I'm not going to pretend about this one. It's going to be hard. Maybe even obscenely impossible for you.

You might've experienced massive pain, misunderstanding, and frustration, which you've categorized as being inflicted by the opposite sex. All of us are showing up with wildly diverse experiences, so I'm not even going to try to imagine what yours might be.

But let's say that you're carrying such enormous pain, pain that you associate with the masculine and all that it has created. Pain that you have no intention of giving up or backing down from anytime soon.

You want this pain to live inside of you so that you don't forget. So that you don't slip up, get weak, and find yourself in the same situation again. You want this pain so bad that you're practically daring it to swallow you, to chew you into bits until there's nothing left of you.

As intense as all that sounds, I get it. I do. I see, hear, feel, and acknowledge your pain, your hurt—the story that lives inside of you.

But at the same time, I want to tell you: you can't let that story own you.

You can't let that pain run the show that is your beautiful life.

It might hurt like hell to let it go, but you must.

You do yourself a crude disservice by holding on to it. It isn't yours to carry forever. It isn't yours to use as a shield. To block any and all forms of love from you.

You were destined for more than that. And if you want to truly step into your feminine power, if you want to truly free yourself from all that's holding you back, you've got to clear up the pain you feel toward "the other side." You've got to let them off the hook. You've got to stop criticizing and start celebrating. You've got to stop thinking the worst and start envisioning the best.

Claim that. It's yours to hold on to.

It's an opportunity to free yourself, and to also free the men who are squinting under the harsh light of your judgments.

Without that harsh light bearing down upon them, I'm telling you: *they will be transformed.*

They will be able to breathe more deeply, to feel into themselves, into who they really are. They will feel the love that flows from you and they will not be able to help themselves; they will radiate that love back. They will keep the cycle of love going, so that it continues, so that it swats down all hindrances to the feminine.

Shower the masculine with love.

Let the love rain down like mad. Just let it go. Liberate it.

The love within you wants to be in motion. Don't restrict it. Don't block it from leaking into certain areas of your life. Let it move, unhindered. Let it elevate and empower all men who cross your path.

The patriarchy is not just antiwoman; its intent is more far-reaching than that. It is against humanity as a whole. It is a system that feeds off of the energy of disempowerment, no matter what its shape or form may be. No matter if it's a man or a woman who's experiencing it.

When we wave the flag of "feminine power," we're waving it for everyone. This isn't some exclusive, limited-seating type of deal. This is our right. This belongs to all of us.

The sooner we can embrace and distill this knowledge, the sooner all of us, men and women, can band together and birth a whole new reality. One where the spirit of the feminine has ample space to stretch its legs, to finally know what it means to be free.

Anjali Mudra

The idea of bringing masculine and feminine energy into harmony throughout our world can be a little overwhelming. It's a daunting task, one that cannot be taken on by you alone, for the healing of humanity in its entirety.

But you can do your part.

You can bring more balance and love to the world by balancing the masculine and feminine energies within yourself.

And you can do this by using a powerful mudra. A mudra is a sacred hand position. It's a Sanskrit word that means "seal."

By moving our hands and fingers into certain positions, we can direct our subtle energy a certain way and allow for a desired outcome to flower within us. There are mudras to help with digestion, sleeping, concentrating, building more energy, balancing the chakras … you name it, there's a mudra for it.

Now, if you want to balance masculine and feminine energy, the anjali mudra is the one to work with. Though you might not be familiar with this name, you have no doubt seen—and maybe even tried—this mudra, many times.

It's a prayer mudra, with your palms pressed together at the level of the heart. By creating this position at the heart, you activate the energies of love. And the coming together of the palms illustrates the coming together of masculine and feminine, in union at the heart.

→ *power exercise for* ←
BALANCING MASCULINE AND FEMININE ENERGY

Preparing for the Exercise

Find a quiet, comfortable place to sit.

Doing the Exercise

The spine should be straight and the chin slightly tucked in toward the chest.

Bring both palms together at the heart and focus your energy there. Feel the innate love radiating in that space.

Breathe deeply through the nose as you stay centered in the heart. Feel your energy pool together. Feel the harmony flooding into your body.

If you'd like, you can also set an intention silently.

You can say, "*The masculine and feminine merge in love.*"

Now, as you inhale, press your palms firmly together. As you exhale, relax your palms, but still keep them touching one another.

Continue the pattern of inhale, press; exhale, release.

Try to keep this practice going for five to ten minutes. You might notice that your brain feels more balanced and clear, as bringing the palms together in this way helps to promote harmony between both brain hemispheres. You might also notice a certain ease and joy bubbling within, as the energies of the masculine and feminine merge and dance with one another.

If it's hard to concentrate, just remember to keep bringing your attention back to the breath and the action that is happening with the palms. Gently call your focus back to the practice, with no judgments or expectations.

⇒ power exercise for ⇐
FORGIVING MEN

It would be near-impossible to truly step into your feminine power without releasing the pain and anger that you might feel toward any specific man, or the masculine in general.

The patriarchy has been destructive to us all, shutting down the potential of both men and women. We've got to start getting real about that fact so that we can rebuild and heal ourselves from the inside out.

Preparing for the Exercise

Find a quiet, comfortable place to sit.

Doing the Exercise

Sit up with a straight spine.

Close your eyes.

Take a few deep breaths to relax yourself.

Envision a sea of men before you.

Feel the energy of the masculine and all that it encompasses before you, and around you as well. In the sea of men, you might see some faces of people you know. Men who've hurt you in the past.

Now breathe deeply, as you imagine you are looking around at all these faces. Taking all of the energy in. It might be a little intense to feel all of this masculine energy, so go slowly.

Now, instead of demonizing this energy, I want you to see the fear that it holds. I want you to see and feel the fear that the masculine has had to endure for so long. Feel the weight of the responsibility they've had to hold. Feel how challenging it must have been for so long to pretend to be strong, infallible; to hide all emotion and compassion. Feel how limiting and deadening that has been to the male spirit. Feel the ways in which that mentality has kept man from really knowing himself.

Next, I want you to imagine that you are feeling beyond the surface of their exteriors. I want you to unmask this crowd of men. I want you to see into them, directly into their souls, where their true essence lies. See the fullness of who they are. See the love and peace and beauty that is inherently there.

Breathe this all the way in.

Feel a sense of deep acceptance and love filling you up. And if you feel any emotion here, express it. Wherever you are with this is where you need to be.

Try to stay with this exercise for as long as you need to! If you have trouble doing this the first time, accept where you're at. This isn't an easy thing to take on. Be patient with yourself, and try to come back to this exercise the next day. And if you feel any anxiety or fear while doing this, it might help not to envision the faces of men you know. If it feels like it's way too much, try visualizing them with generic faces. This should bring some of the intensity down.

→ *affirmation for* ←
THE MASCULINE

I see evidence of the divine in all men,
And in all things masculine,
Everywhere I go.

I feel the ancient knowing
That exists in all men.
I feel the ways in which all men
Connect and integrate within my own being.

I know the pain of all men,
And the ways in which they've expressed that pain.
I cherish and value every man,
Even during the moments when fear clouds
His unique and vibrant essence,
Just as it does with me and all women.

I open my heart to all men,
I see all men as sacred expressions
Worthy of love.
I see the masculine in them
Uniting to merge with the feminine in me,
And in every woman.

I carry this vision in my breath,
And in my every cell.
I feel the heart of man and woman
Merging in peace, in love.

THE HEART DOESN'T NEED PROTECTION

CAN I LET YOU in on a little secret?

Whenever I first begin working with a woman client, I almost always start out by working with her heart chakra. That's because I know that the heart is where the breakthroughs happen. Whatever her reasons may be for booking the session, I know that the work we do with the heart will support her.

That's because, when the energies of love are liberated, a woman becomes a high-vibrating goddess whose every breath calls the world to her. Just by expanding and opening the heart (through breath work, visualization, and movement) I've seen women attract partners, suddenly get that dream job they've been hoping for, heal from a past hurt, and even experience a state of pleasure that they never thought was possible.

I know how essential it is for a woman to open her heart energy. When a woman isn't operating from the heart, the fierce life force within her withers down to nothing. Because the heart is the nucleus of a woman. She is powered by love.

It is the force that moves her through life, whether it's the whirlwind romance, or motherhood, or being of service to others. Maybe it's starting her own business for the sake of making people's lives better. Maybe it's what compels her decision to drop everything to take care of a sick parent. Whatever it is, love is there to carry her through, to articulate itself in the flurry of activity that makes up her life.

But then there are those craters in the road that throw her off course. These are the things that smash her heart up into bits: *The bad breakup, the divorce, the loss of someone who meant the world to her. The injustice. The brutality of other people, of systems, of nature.*

As the heartbreaks continue to pile up in a woman's life, she might decide that it's best to start building walls, to start shielding the thing that fuels her. It's a rough world out there and her heart needs protection. So she covers it up.

She blocks off all of the joyful energy that so naturally emanates from it. She starts to live with a bit more caution.

Maybe with the next potential lover she meets, she takes it slow. She displays coldness when she feels heat. She reveals fragments of her true nature when she feels a desire to gush and flow. She becomes a tight, manufactured display of restrictions.

She holds herself back the majority of the time.

She speaks in half sentences, looks down at the ground to avoid eye contact.

She does this a little more each day. And she very slowly begins the process of disentangling herself from the heart.

Losing connection to the heart, for a woman, is like losing the ability to breathe. It is a retreat from life. It is taking down the sail and locking the boat away when there are still more adventures to be had.

Your heart is the essence of what you are. It springs you into inspired action. It gives you the space to embody your higher, divine qualities. You must not ever shut the valve to your love space down.

If you do have walls around your heart, I know it might be tough, goddess sister; but whenever you're ready, you can be free again. You can reclaim your heart space.

The people around you need it.

And, of course, so do you.

You Weren't Created Just for the Hell of It

Whenever heartbreak makes its appearance in your life, you must beckon for your courage and your strength. Because there is too much at stake here.

If you become shut down in the heart, this world loses you. It loses your signature blend of radiance.

You are needed at this time.

If you weren't, you wouldn't be breathing right now.

You wouldn't be here.

A woman like you is not created just for the hell of it.

A woman like you has work to do, love to spread, people to lift up.

There is a purpose for you. In your breath, and in your blood, and in your cells, the blueprint of that purpose is vibrating.

Close your eyes and tune in to it. Let the vibration of that purpose fill you up. Feel the vibration of that purpose and the way it corresponds with love.

Love streams through you in endless waves. It is there, always, undiluted and pure. Through your waking states, through your sleeping states, through your states of superconscious euphoria—love lives and moves within you. It cannot be encumbered by walls or any other blockages.

Even as you aim to close it off, you will still feel it.

It will call to you during those moments when your guard is down. It will whisper in your ear and make the hairs on the back of your neck stand up. It will continue to vibrate and burn inside of you, even as you try to forget. Even as you concern yourself with other things.

The biggest mistake women make when thinking about love is looking at it as something outside of themselves. Love is not a wild goose chase. It's not a long-winded journey that involves great distances. You don't have to overturn every rock. You don't have to wait by the windowsill with your eyes full of longing. You don't have to find the perfect man that will be every last thing you ever dreamed he would be.

That is not the path to love. In fact, there is no path. There is just you and the love that you carry everywhere you go.

To access it, you just have to breathe, here and now. Imagine each breath melting away all the layers of protection that have been fused to the heart and feel your love space crack open again.

It may feel vulnerable and messy.

You may feel suddenly exposed.

The voice of fear may try to reason with you, telling you that it isn't safe to put yourself out there again.

But your job is not to listen to it. If you listen to that voice, if you follow your fear, you will shrink back and retreat behind the thick, velvety wall of complacency.

So you must stay awake.

Remember, always, that the heart is your fuel.

→ power tips for ← DESTROYING THE WALLS AROUND THE HEART

As you move and unfold your magic in the world, feel the magnitude of the heart propelling you forward.

As you speak, imagine that the words coming out of your mouth are humble servants of the heart; feel the way the words reverberate off the root of your mouth.

Take in every sight around you as if you were looking through your heart, and start to notice beauty in the most unexpected places.

By doing this, you will wake up a fever in you.

There will be a hunger there that you never knew existed. When the heart is open, and when it is used to experience all aspects of life, there is a natural joy that opens up. It emanates from you; it pours out in everything that you do.

This will be the thing that changes the world.

⇥ badass self-care for ⇤
THE HEART

The heart is the part of woman that is most raw. It is aching with the tender energies of love and expansion.

It is your way in. The place from which you draw out all forms and forces.

And it gets beat up a lot.

As strong and powerful as you are, your heart will get hurt in this life. Many times over.

You know this; it is something that you've always understood. In fact, you've also always understood, at some level, that through this hurt that inevitably presses its way in, your power gets sharpened.

Your heart, like a muscle, strengthens. Regardless of what comes to it. Pain or pleasure. Heartache or joy. With each sensation that it fully takes on, that it wraps its arms around, carefree like a child, it grows at a level of even deeper courageousness.

The awareness in you expands thousandfold.

The heart is like some vibrant, pumping miracle, wildly aware of its worth.

And even so, it needs to be cared for. Self-care for the heart is absolutely essential. For the heart is always working for us, always transmuting energies and penetrating new layers and depths.

To keep it shining in its radiance, we must practice a little badass self-care for the heart. Here's a great exercise that will make your love space tingle.

⇒ *badass self-care ritual for* ⇐
THE HEART

Preparing for the Exercise

This exercise is simple to do and you can practice it anywhere, even when you're out at the grocery store or stuck waiting for a delayed plane in a crowded airport. Do this in any position that's comfortable.

Doing the Exercise

The most effective (and fun) way I know of practicing self-care for the heart is through what I like to call *breast breathing*.

Take an invigorating inhale through the mouth. And instead of imagining that you are breathing down deep into your belly, imagine that you are sending the breath down into your breasts.

The only trick is that you want to send the breath down to both breasts. So once it hits the top of the breasts, you want to envision the breath breaking off into two separate breaths. That way, one breath goes into the left breast and the other breath goes into the right breast.

So to break that down again: As you inhale down, it's one breath/one path. And as soon as the breath reaches the breasts, break it up into two breaths/two paths. And you want to bring the two breaths/two paths all the way to the inside of the breasts behind the nipples.

Then, exhale through the mouth and imagine both breaths moving out of the breasts and joining together to form one breath as it comes up and out of the mouth.

It's the same thing, except in reverse.

Enjoy practicing this for five to ten minutes, and it will revive and refuel your heart energies. Try to make this one a regular practice if you can; it works wonders for aligning you to your feminine, opening up your sensuality and pleasure, and clearing out any stagnant energies that the heart might be holding on to.

A warning for when you do this one, though: You might feel a tingling, soul-opening sensation that changes the whole game for you and puts you in deep union with your fierce woman-power. So only proceed if you're ready to own it.

SECTION IV
⇒ SPIRIT ⇐

YOU DON'T NEED A CRYSTAL BALL TO ACCESS YOUR INNER MYSTIC

I'LL NEVER FORGET THE night a friend and I took a drive to San Francisco. The city was about forty miles away from where we lived. We had no real plans, no specific destination. Just a desire to be in the city, amidst the noise and the lights.

When we arrived, the electricity in the air was palpable. We walked the streets, drinking it all in.

In the middle of our walk, we heard the faint sounds of music. As if we were one person, my friend and I stopped walking at the exact same time, almost hypnotized by this sound. It was coming from the inside of a jazz bar. We gave each other a look and nodded.

"Let's go in," my friend said, already moving toward the door.

We took seats at a corner table. Ordered some appetizers and drinks. We were only nineteen at the time, so it was just tea and coffee for us.

At the front of the room, there was this four- or five-piece jazz band. The sound coming from them was like something from a dream. They were playing lots of classical standards: Billie Holiday and Louis Armstrong–type stuff. I was a huge jazz fan at the time and knew all of the songs by heart.

After they had played half a dozen songs, the saxophone player looked out at the room.

"Anyone have a request?" he asked. He looked right at me and my friend.

Stunned that he was addressing us, I just sat there for a moment. After being consumed so deeply by the music for the last half hour, it was like being snapped out of a reverie. My friend must have felt the same way, because she remained quiet too.

In my head, I heard myself saying the words "Georgia on My Mind."

It was one of my favorite songs at the time, and I was aching to hear it. However, I felt kind of shy about shouting out the name of the song across the room. So I continued to remain silent.

"Nothing?" the musician asked the room. "All right."

He shrugged. And with a smile, he muttered something to the rest of his bandmates. And then they started to play the next song. And from the very first note, the hairs on my arms started to stand up.

Because they were actually playing "Georgia on My Mind." The song I had requested. In my head.

I turned to my friend with wide eyes. And before I could get the words out, she said, rather excitedly, "Oh my god, I wanted to request that song, but I didn't say anything!"

And I was like, "Are you kidding me? *I* wanted to request that song!"

We both looked at each other in disbelief for a moment or two before we turned back to the musicians, eager to continue hearing the song that both of us had mentally requested without the other knowing.

That night has always stood out to me. It was a magical experience. One that revealed to me just how powerful women truly are, especially when they come together. Just by harboring a desire in our minds, we made it into a reality—and we didn't have to take a single action.

Now, I'm not advocating the idea that we need not take action on the things we want to translate into reality. The marriage of thought and action can be insanely fruitful. However, what happened at the jazz bar that night was proof to me that women are mystical beings capable of absolutely anything they put their minds to.

All of us have an inner mystic within.

What Is the Inner Mystic, Exactly?

The inner mystic is an invisible, magical force that deeply embodies the Source or the Creator. It is not tethered down to this earthly form of life. This force knows how to create, how to activate the energies of deep wisdom and knowing, and how to travel between and interact with all realms, physical or otherwise.

That inner mystic is at work all the time.

She's there when you visualize something into existence.

She's there when you are thinking of a person and then, minutes later, they call.

She's there when you dream about something that happens days later.

She's there when you feel the presence of a deceased loved one nearby.

She's there when you have visions, when you see things that are not tied down to this physical plane of existence.

She's there when you know things, *you just know them*, and you can't explain why.

Your inner mystic is a gift. One you must keep unwrapping, again and again, throughout your whole life. The more you unwrap her, the more of a connection you will establish to her. With stunning clarity, she will guide and protect you like no other. She will make you feel comforted in the fact that this is not all there is. Your inner mystic ties you to the nonphysical realms from which you came.

And she is not to be feared.

Too many of us fear that this connection is otherworldly, or it is not in alignment with our religious or philosophical beliefs, and we shut it down. I come in contact with many women who feel like they shouldn't have access to this deep connection with their inner mystic, because it's none of their business to tap this deep source of power.

But let me tell you something: it is your business.

You are mystical. You are of the divine and all that is. The abilities of the inner mystic are natural to who you are; this is something that goes beyond the comprehension of the physical mind and body that you temporarily possess. Anybody who has made you feel like a freak for becoming entangled with your inner mystic doesn't truly understand you and the gifts that you are here to shine on this planet.

Many women have been denied their power because the people around them have made them feel as if their relationship with all things unseen is somehow wrong. Hundreds of reasons have been fabricated to squash this goddess-given ability. Take your pick; here are some I've heard:

- It's evil and it's of the devil, so stop doing it.

- That's weird. You're weird. It can't be true. You're just being weird.

- That was nothing special. It was just a coincidence.

- You really shouldn't be messing with this stuff. You need to go to church more.

- Whoa. So you've turned into a New Age hippie all of a sudden. When did that happen?

- Women think they know everything!

- Yup. Uh-huh. Are you on your period?

Complete silence is also another one.

When you're trying to share a bit about your inner mystic and what you've experienced, the listener just blinks. And keeps their mouth shut. They have absolutely nothing to say, because the whole thing intimidates, terrifies, disturbs, or annoys them in some way. So they just keep their mouth shut. The silence is meant to detract you from the path of wild knowing.

But the path of wild knowing is the one that is calling to your heart. I know this because you're reading these words right now.

To pursue the path of wild knowing, every woman must surrender to the wisdom of the inner mystic within. She is waiting for you. She is longing for the moment when you open your heart to her and allow her to move through you.

What does this mean exactly? How can you become more open to your inner mystic?

⇒ power tips for ⇐
AWAKENING YOUR INNER MYSTIC

First, start with the times when you get the intuitive hits.

When you have a feeling about something, don't ignore it. Take it all the way in and let it intermingle with your cells. Feel it from the top to the bottom. Soak in it.

As you start to do this more, you will find your intuitive abilities deepening, and perhaps giving you more than just little bits and pieces of information here and there. It will start to flow like a continuous stream.

Record your dreams as well. Try to understand the deeper meaning that is present within them.

And when you want to manifest something out of thin air, let your inner mystic lead the way. Raise the vibration of your thoughts, and be confident in your visualizations of all that you desire.

When you have visions about something, write them down. Seek to find the connections between them and what is happening in your own life.

Share your inner mystic powers with people who will understand them. Don't let anyone cheapen this magic that you contain within, this portal you have to Source.

Let your inner mystic come alive with everything you do. Feel as if you are being held by a force, by a creative and loving energy that is greater than yourself, but that reflects and contains all of the beauty that you carry within.

Most importantly: Drown out any and all disapproval from others. Stay true to the natural gifts that you carry within. Use those gifts to light the world anew.

ACCEPT WHAT IS, EVEN WHEN THINGS ARE MESSY

———

I LOVE WRITING IN cafés. Something about the ambience.

A good cafe offers the comfort of a womb, swelling with possibilities. Velvety tones from various voices, in all directions. Laptop screens illuminating words that fill up so many pages. And the smell of coffee, like a promise, lingering in the air. It's as if the combination of all these elements were somehow conspiring to illicit the powers of concentration, creativity, and romance. I, for one, would be utterly lost without a café within walking distance.

During one of my café sessions, from a year ago, I remember this couple sitting at the table next to me. The seating in this particular place was tight, so the couple was literally *right there*. Meaning I could very clearly hear every word of their conversation.

And the words I heard were quite painful.

Apparently, the couple was on a blind date. And things were not flowing between them. The awkwardness was so bad I nearly choked on my own saliva listening to them.

Although I couldn't help but overhear this awkward encounter, I felt guilty somehow. It was as if I had been granted front row seats to witnessing something very private, like the final argument before someone decides to file the divorce papers or the mental breakdown of some beloved public figure.

I looked around the crowded café, hoping to find a spot to move to. But there were no other tables left. So I remained in my seat and kept on working. I finally had to mentally tell myself, *Hey, it's not my fault I'm overhearing every word! It's their fault no one's taking the initiative and calling it a night!*

The guy was telling the woman all kinds of mundane details about his elderly mother and his teenage children. He was talking about foods he liked to eat in excruciatingly exhaustive detail.

And the woman was sitting there, coldly muttering "Uh-huh" at the end of his every sentence. Every now and then, she'd throw him a bone and ask a question. But it was obvious that her heart wasn't into it.

By the end, the guy kept repeating, "This was good! This was good!" over and over again, as if trying to convince them both that the evening was not a total disaster.

"We have to do this again. We have to," he said, as things were winding down. I couldn't see her face, but it sounded like the woman was smirking when she responded.

The strange thing was that her exit was slow. You would've figured that a woman responding in that way would bolt out of there in a heartbeat. But she didn't. She took her time. She humored him. Threw in a few extra questions for good measure. In some strange way, it was as if she was waiting for something, anything, to alter the temperature of that evening encounter.

But that something never happened.

He asked her, one last time, for another date, and she kind of shrugged.

She eventually walked off, after a stiff handshake and a tight smile. Minutes later, even though both of them had left the café, this stark feeling of awkwardness continued to linger in the air.

Some things are just not meant to be. Both of these people truly wanted to connect with somebody, otherwise they wouldn't have gone on the blind date in the first place. But even with the best of intentions, their meeting fell flat on its face. You can't fake connection. You can't force things that aren't meant to happen.

And yet we force so many things, so much of the time.

We push during the times when we should be stepping back and assessing. Or abandoning something altogether.

Cycles Stop for No One

The energy of feminine power, of women, runs in cycles.

The power of nature is intermingled deep within our blood. We are the physical embodiment of life, death, and rebirth. Our life force depends upon our ability to navigate through all of these cycles, accepting all that is, no matter what comes next.

When we stay stuck in one mode for too long, we suffer.

This world says to stay in the mode of act, force, strive, push. That's a very masculine approach. The masculine approach says that you deserve to have everything you want now. Not in the next hour or in the next day. But now. It says to force your way through, even when things don't feel right. Even when the chemistry's not there. Even when all the pieces don't add up completely.

This is a very toxic recipe. We're living in the age of "Ram Things Through." And the RTT age is not something that resonates with the natural ways of being a woman and embodying the feminine. This is why so many women feel inadequate and unable to keep up with the demands of life.

We're out of breath, running like mad to keep it all together, wondering why we're feeling so winded. We try to be the ultimate superwoman, strive to be the best in every area of our lives. But this isn't possible.

You can't do everything. You. Just. Can't.

You can't force every aspect of your life into polished perfection. And that doesn't mean that you're inadequate.

In fact, your adequacy is at its brightest when you are simply doing nothing. Just by being present and breathing and feeling through every sensation in your body, you are adequate. You are beyond adequate.

Everything you ever wanted for yourself, you already embody in your natural state. That is you at your most powerful. That is you, giving the ego permission to take a break so that your inner goddess can do her thing. Accepting the reality of this moment, here and now—that is all it takes.

Know this: The feminine approach is vastly different from the masculine. It isn't based on the idea that you should have everything you want right this second.

The feminine way says everything you could ever want or need is within you already. The keys to the castle are at your disposal, and they always have been. You just have to decide to reach for them so that you can unlock the treasures that are waiting within you.

Yes, there are times in life when pushing through is appropriate. But it's about knowing when those times are. It's about navigating through your cycles and accepting where things are in this moment so that you trust yourself in doing exactly what needs to be done.

When you force something into fruition, don't be surprised if, somewhere down the line, things start to fall apart. Let's say that the man and woman on the blind date met for a second time, and then a third. At some point during this whole charade, things would have to go south; it would just be a matter of when.

The man in this scenario was perfectly willing to force the illusion of connection by expressing his desire to continue something that obviously wasn't working out. But the woman, with her silence and shrugging, wasn't having it. She wasn't willing to force something out of nothing. Instead, she allowed her feminine to lead her, and in doing so, she saved herself from investing extra time, energy, and attention into someone she wasn't crazy about.

→ power tips for ←
ACCEPTING, NOT FORCING

If something isn't clicking, if you've been pouring sweat and tears into something that is deadening your spirit, if you are pounding the pavement of a path that just, in the pit of your stomach, does not sit right with you, that's your cue to step away. If stepping away seems scary to you, then don't abandon it completely. Just make a plan to put the thing down for a while so that you can breathe and think clearly about what you truly want for yourself right now.

Whatever you do, listen to yourself. The feminine energies within are longing to be heard by you. Accept what is in this moment and you will know the true meaning of bliss.

CALL IN YOUR SISTERS

IT WAS FALL. RED leaves were trickling from the trees.

Inside of a café, a dear friend and I were sipping tea. A conversation about our disappointment with the current state of politics led to an even deeper conversation. One about women, about all of the structures that have thrown water over our fire. We talked about the systems that have oppressed our spirits, that have driven us to hate and shame our bodies, to lower our voices and keep our heads down.

Then the conversation veered into unwanted sexual advances from men.

I told my friend about a time when I was just sixteen. I was playing piano at home in an upstairs room by myself. A family friend who was visiting appeared in the doorway of the room. He had droopy eyes and smelled of ointment and dishrags. I had always felt severe discomfort around him. The guy was in his seventies, and I noticed that whenever there was nobody looking, he would give me a kind of look. A look that no man in his seventies should be giving a teenage girl.

And now here he was. In the doorway. Grinning. Nodding his head in tune with every note I played.

I glanced up briefly, then looked back down at my hands, at the keys. Trying to signal that I wasn't interested in chitchat. Or anything that had to do with this guy, for that matter.

Not taking the hint (or maybe he took the hint and just didn't give a shit), this guy sat down on the bench next to me. And very quickly, as if he had been building up to this moment for months, he placed his rough and gigantic hands over mine.

"This is how you play it," he muttered, trying to bring my hands to the right keys.

I froze. My hands, my fingers, were locked tight. I held my breath, trying to cut the scent of ointment and dishrags off at the pass.

He proceeded to sensually rub my hands. Looked into my eyes, waiting for my reaction. Hungering for it, by the looks of it.

This story that I told my friend ended with me pulling my hands away and storming out of the room. I never spoke about what happened to anyone.

It was a disturbing encounter that I had, for the most part, not thought about too much. By not speaking of it, I figured that I was scrubbing it clean from the record. Like it never existed. Like that line had never been crossed.

But on that fall day with my friend, I divulged. Told her about how I felt. How embarrassed and ashamed I was. How I didn't feel comfortable telling anybody about it because it had been so awkward and so wrong.

My friend listened to me, openly and with love. We connected deeply that afternoon as we both continued to share these kinds of experiences with one another.

A couple of hours later, while I was at home washing the dishes, something happened. A thought struck me like a thunderbolt. I put down the glass that I was washing and looked out the window.

I had just realized something.

There was more to the story than I had told my friend.

After the man's hand rubbing, I hadn't had the opportunity to storm away. Not just yet.

While caressing my hands, this guy then proceeded to lean toward me and press his humongous, wet lips against my own. Kissing me, as he softly shut his eyes.

My insides were turning, screaming with panic, but on the outside, I remained silent. Then I stood up from the creaky piano bench and stormed out of the room.

After that, I don't exactly remember how I reasoned my way through what had occurred. It was too uncomfortable to process and fully welcome into my being. I didn't want anyone to know about it. I didn't even want myself to know about it, apparently. There was nothing in my language and understanding that could help me to grapple with this.

And now, to realize that I had locked away this very upsetting detail of the kiss somewhere inside of me was quite astounding. It is amazing what the mind can do when it feels that it cannot process something.

I texted my friend, right after the realization.

Wrote to her about how I remembered the kiss and how I had buried the memory inside of myself for two whole decades. It made me think: how many others out there have shut down all the details of their own personal experiences? The ones that saddened them. That disrupted their sense of self. That made them feel like there was no one in the world who could ever know, who could ever truly understand.

My friend's deep and loving ability to witness me, to hear my story, created the space. It liberated the secret that I carried inside of me. It held me in its arms, in a deep sense of safety and nonjudgment, so that I could remember. So that I could heal, release, transform. Be more of the woman that I am meant to be.

That is the power of sisterhood.

It is a culture defined by love—and death-defying amounts of trust. When women gather, the world around them bends and shifts; everything is transformed.

One woman alone is packed with so much power. Imagine two. Or twenty. Or a hundred. All aligned to the same purpose. All working in divine unity, expressing love and compassion with a stunning kind of ease, like it was as simple as taking the next breath.

For Your Visualizing Pleasure

Stop a moment and imagine that there are spaces created to support the coming together of women, across all lines—cultural, religious, sexual, political.

In parks, gardens, cafés, community centers, the corners of high-rise offices, the back rooms of yoga studios or libraries.

Imagine women having places that they can always go, where the energy pooled reflects the magnitude of their inner "she" worlds; a place where they can go to be nourished and soothed. Intermingling their energy with that of other women. Expressing the things that have sat, like boulders, within them for too long.

With a space like this, a woman who experiences any kind of upset would know that drowning in her pain wasn't an option. She could always count on an empowering space out there, waiting for her, its door always open. She would know that her sisters were there to listen, to witness and embrace the truth of what she is.

In this kind of world, women wouldn't have to suffocate in silence or struggle to remedy challenges on their own. There would be no lines of separation drawn in the ground, keeping us immobile and cut off from one another.

Wouldn't that be amazing?

Stop Competing and Start Co-Creating

This myth of division has persisted for way too long.

There's this idea out there that promotes pitting yourself against the other woman—whether it's for a man, or a job, or simply determining who has the more knockout body. We get stuck playing this game, telling ourselves that this is what matters, that this is how we should motivate and inspire ourselves to be truly great. To define our worth.

But instead, this does the exact opposite. That's because when you're consumed with competing, judging, and criticizing the women who you should be embracing as your sisters, you emit a tangible frequency of fear.

This fear starts to color everything that you do. It makes you feel as if you are constantly being driven to prove that you are worthy and amazing. It's almost as if the more you fear, the more this gaping hole inside of you widens. You start to feel unfulfilled. You look out at the women around you and long for those sacred connections. That is because there is something inside all of us that knows how wildly essential sisterhood is to our hearts, our bodies, and our spirits.

And its value isn't just about gaining support during tough times. Sisterhood is also for the good times as well. It's for sharing laughter, for celebrating wins, for expressing joy, for swapping stories, for inciting action, for holding each other accountable. Sisterhood reminds us that we are whole and complete, just the way we are. It also serves as a channel for accumulating massive amounts of feminine energy.

When we combine forces, weaving feminine energy together—an energy that has, for many years, been denied its power and made to feel weaker—the vibration of that energy moves. It is fueled by life force energy, and that life force energy flows out to touch everything in sight, to animate and imbue the world in a kind of delirious splendor.

That energy is there to tap and to embody. So that even when women disband, when they go their separate ways to tend to their lives, there's still that feeling of connection. There's still that sense of feminine power, sitting firm yet gentle in the belly, affirming to us that we are more powerful than we could ever know.

That power gets taken with us everywhere we go. We project it from our eyes, from the words we speak. The universe smiles and hums as a result.

When my friend's warm and radiant presence set the stage, allowing for me to dig up something that I didn't even know was there, I was absolutely astounded. The mystical nature of the feminine is drenched in such power. There's a magical quality there, one that seems vast and endless, ever-expansive. Just when I truly believe that I've got it, I realize that I'm mistaken. There's always more to get. There's always room to move forward, to make even more space for the bold ease that is the feminine.

Let's all focus on uplifting and empowering one another.

Pave the walkways and construct the bridges that the other women in your life can walk across. Project love and withhold fear. Welcome the ferocious force that is sisterhood into your heart. Don't let the judgment and the fear keep you from evolving your relationships. Raise your vibration higher than that.

➤ power tips for ◄
CREATING SISTERHOOD

One thing you can do right away: start by nurturing a space for sisterhood in your life. Get your own "Feminine Power Circle" together. It could be held at your home or in a public spot. Invite a few friends to come out and share sacred space together. It doesn't have to be formal. In some ways, striving toward formality could set you back from actually meeting.

Just aim for authenticity. For showing up and being real.

Create a container together. Forge a circle, no matter how small, where you can express, share, support, and listen. Reach your arms and your heart out toward the women around you. Treat each other as holy, powerful goddesses who deserve all the beauty and joy that their hearts can carry.

This small act will not be insignificant. This small act will pave the way toward acceptance and understanding of the feminine, and all the women who represent it.

RAISE YOUR VIBRATION, EVEN WHEN OTHERS ARE DEPLETING YOU

You KNOW THAT FEELING when you're around a certain person and you suddenly feel drained and depleted?

Your high-vibrating energy plummets to the ground, and you're left feeling low and uninspired, wondering why you even bothered to talk to this person in the first place. I've been there many times. And I finally figured out how to combat it: keep my energy vibrating so high, so fierce, so full force, that absolutely nothing can knock it down.

Read on and you'll learn how to do this.

Vibrate High, Regardless

Your essence was carved from the highest of vibrations. The magnetic frequencies of your heart. The steady pulsing beneath your skin. The light that radiates behind the pupils of your eyes, revealing a sliver of the mystery within.

You were made to burn bright. To radiate at the highest level. To take the form of a living, breathing three-dimensional goddess; one who transforms the space around her by simply being who she is, at her fullest and most courageous.

This becomes a tricky thing to do when people in our lives are challenging us, detracting from the vibrancy of who we really are.

Where things should flow, where love should dominate, there is strain and never-ending frustration.

If there is someone in your life who is draining and depleting you, sucking dry all reserves of energy and frequency from your being, you've got to step up. Your vibration, your Shakti, is being downgraded, lowered to a state that isn't what you are.

Think of all the love and intention that it took to create your vibrant being. That love and intention would like to be expressed through you and every single thing that you do, no matter how mundane you might think it to be.

When you're allowing the forces around you to determine your fate, to dictate what your vibration is, you are doing yourself a deep disservice. You are allowing for the force of your being to sink into the background and hide the awe-inspiring beauty that encompasses what you are.

If you'd like to keep your vibration high, you have to come to the table already grounded in it. You've got to harness and cultivate that energy so that no matter what happens, you're in the zone. You're swimming in the waves of deep power, love, and acceptance. Without a life jacket or a care in the world. Cause when you're in that place, nothing can touch the frequency of what you are. You sit at the heart of the eternal when you're there. You melt in such a way that you merge into the every-thingness that throbs at the core of all that is.

People in our lives are going to test us. They're going to challenge us. Our relationships are here to grow us into our truest selves. To give us permission to step fully into the vibration of love so that we can express the depths of our beings.

We must learn to surrender to the madness and the love and the chaos and the deep connection that transpires in our every relationship. We must start to understand that the people who are hurting or frustrating us are on their own journeys and have their own very unique lessons to learn in this life. When you raise your vibration high, not only are you protecting yourself from their low energy, but you are actually raising their energy as well.

That's the thing about high vibration. It's irresistible. So much so that any form or structure that encounters it will raise a notch or two just to keep up. This is an effortless kind of act that does not really involve any conscious thought. Just you, in your power, projecting the inner truth of your light.

Your vibration—the divine feminine power in you—is a sacred gift. Take it into your arms. Live through it. Use it and you will become capable of stunning feats. You will gain the ability to tie the barrels of guns into knots with your own bare hands.

The higher your vibration, the more difficult it will be for another to drag it down. You won't feel the energy suck, the heaviness of the company that you're with. And they will unmistakably feel uplifted by your presence.

Stop Punching Fear in the Face.
Do This Instead ...

Fear is the biggest vibration-killer of all time. Don't forget that. If you've been battling with fear for what feels like centuries and nothing ever works, put down your sword, warrioress!

Instead of focusing so much on smoking out the fear, lean toward the feeling of love. Whereas fear is the lowest vibration, love is the highest. Penetrate the membrane of love within you. Step into it. Drink it in through your nostrils. Feel it throughout your being. When you start living from a deep place of love, there's no room for the fear. Fear becomes unnecessary. It's too low for your being to even bother getting caught up in. Be with the love, full force. Head on. In love, there is power.

If someone is ravaging your vibration to bits, remember that fear is the thing that compels them. By beaming the love right into the face of fear, that someone won't feel motivated to pursue the same level of attack on your energy. The love coming out of you will elevate them.

And in the end, it's up to you if you think that physically being next to/in the same room as this person isn't serving your highest good. Maybe they're a danger to you—physically or emotionally—and you just can't be in their sphere any longer. You have a right to protect your energy by making yourself more unavailable (or even completely unavailable), giving them fewer opportunities to get their hooks in you. But do this from a place of love. If you attempt to cut ties from a place of rage or bitterness, then your vibration will continue to stay low.

Just because you're removing someone from your life doesn't mean that you're removing the emotion.

The anger, the frustration, the fear—all of that belongs to you. It isn't tied up in another person or circumstance. You must channel your energies with loving intention so you don't get stuck with a pile full of tumultuous feelings in the end.

Ideally, you will call forth the love in you so forcefully that all the magic that you are will inspire the highest of vibrations out of the people, and the world, around you. Stay rooted in your being and nothing will be able to knock you down ever again.

➔ power exercise for ←
ELEVATING AND PROTECTING YOUR VIBRATION

Preparing for the Exercise

This one requires standing. If it's difficult to stand, you can also do it from a seated position; just remember to keep your spine straight.

Doing the Exercise

1. Stand tall. Elevate your chin up slightly. Make sure your shoulders are relaxed and your spine is straight.

2. Take a deep inhale through puckered lips, as if you are sipping the breath straight through a straw.

3. When you exhale, make the sound "HAA-AAAAAAA." Extend that sound for as long as your exhale can go, as you focus below your navel, deep into your belly. Almost as if

you are speaking this sound into your belly.
Feel the way it reverberates within, the way it
echoes, the way it wakes up and elevates your
vibration. Do this at least five to ten times.

This is a great one to use whenever you know you're
walking into a situation where your vibration will inevitably take a dip. You can also do this first thing in the
morning, to give yourself that foundation of power up
front. You'll notice the difference right away.

Extra Badass Tip:

To keep your vibration as high as you can, cultivate magical thoughts.

Feed your mind with power by placing positive words,
images, mantras, and affirmations around your home.

Eat whole, natural foods that are plant-based and
brimming with all kinds of radiant frequencies.

Step out in nature daily, where the vibration is off the
charts, and be sure to breathe the energy all the way in.

Pamper yourself whenever you can.

Think, speak, see, and feel love wherever you go.

Imagine your being as a magnet for all positive, life-
affirming energies.

Let yourself be an unstoppable force of divine feminine power, and notice everything and everyone around
you rising to meet the kiss of your sweet vibration.

THE COURAGEOUS
ART OF FORGIVING

SOME YEARS BACK, I decided to write a letter to myself about all the things that I forgave myself for. I remember writing, like a madwoman, just letting it all pour out. I forgave myself for all the negative self-talk and all the mistakes I've ever made. I forgave myself for all the times I ever questioned my worth or let fear hold me back from living in my fullest expression.

And let me tell you: by the time that exercise was over, I felt as if I had set down a thousand tons of bricks.

The power of forgiving oneself must not be overlooked.

Before we can even begin to forgive the other people in our lives, we must start with ourselves. We must go within and uproot all of the negativity, blame, or criticism we've inflicted upon the self. As women, we've stretched ourselves in so many ways, tied ourselves up in so many knots, to strive to become who we think we're supposed to be. We've hidden our true feelings, emotions, and opinions for the sake of conforming to the standard. All the while, inside, feeling the lie, feeling the lack of alignment.

But we must let all of that go and forgive ourselves for past mistakes, so that we can move forward. Then we can begin to do the work of forgiving others.

Make Forgiveness an Ongoing Practice

There is nothing more badass than the ability to forgive.

When resentment's the brew filling your cup, there's not a whole lot of space to put anything else. All of the dreams that you'd like to nurture into fruition, all of the love and peace and ease that you'd like to cultivate for yourself—the body will have a tough time holding all of these things if it is also holding on to fear, anger, and resentment.

Think about it: the more time you put into being unable to forgive yourself or others, the less time you will have to create, to feel joy, to feel passion, to explore, and to love.

The inability to forgive—and I'm talking about others and yourself here—is the ultimate vibration-zapper. You might think you're good, that you've got this, that everything's going to be just fine. You might think that you can move on with your life without the weight of this thing impacting you. But that's the ego seducing you into believing that. That's the ego steering the ship.

And the ego should never steer the ship. A woman guided by her ego is a woman whose soul essence has been carved out. She is devoid of heart, fire, creativity, sensuality, and spirit. She forgets the wildness in her, the ability to be like water and to flow.

Forgiveness is a gift you give yourself. It's a willingness to see the person who has wronged you as sacred—and also as human.

All of us are going to screw things up every now and then! It's part of our process here on earth. By forgiving another, you're accepting and acknowledging the idea that every single person on this planet is worthy, no matter what mistakes they've made.

Now, this doesn't mean that the person you forgive is allowed to text you all day or have dinner with you every Friday night. You still get to have boundaries. Forgiving someone doesn't do away with all that. You can forgive someone, yet decide to see them half as much or not at all, if that's what you feel in your heart.

At the end of the day, the inability to forgive means that you are withholding love. Stop keeping love away from yourself, and from others. Let your fierce woman spirit be free of the burden that comes with carrying resentments.

⇥ power affirmation for ⇤
FORGIVING YOURSELF

Breathe. And speak these words from your heart as you read them:

> *I love and accept who I am.*
> *I am in awe and wonder*
> *Of the marvel that I am.*
> *I feel the sacredness of my being.*
> *I feel my inner wisdom burning within.*
> *I feel my body's natural ease,*
> *And its ability to create and transform.*
> *I feel the peace that hums across my every cell.*
> *And I am ready to forgive myself*

Of all mistakes
Of all the times I've doubted my worth
Of the times when I've judged and criticized myself
Of the times when I've withheld love from myself
I let all that go now.
So that I can truly cherish the beauty of who I am.
I am worthy of forgiveness.

Extra Badass Tip:

After the affirmation, grab your journal or paper and a pen and write out all the things you forgive yourself for. Really let it all flow.

→ power tips for ← FORGIVING SOMEONE ELSE

When you do forgive someone, you don't even have to call the person on the phone or send them a card. If it's too difficult for you to make direct contact, you can forgive them right where you are. You don't have to talk to them directly. The intention is enough.

You can meditate on forgiving them. You can say the words aloud to them, as if they are right in front of you. You can write a letter of forgiveness, then do a little ritual where you burn it and then bury it in the earth.

You can chant about it, journal about it.

You can run twenty miles and say "I forgive _____" over and over in your head, like a kind of mantra.

And sometimes it's about having that conversation. Sometimes it's about healing the relationship and finally seeing each other after a decade of not speaking.

You've got to do what works for you. Whatever speaks to the vibration that's nestled in the linings of your heart. Only you know what that is, goddess. You know what you need. And if you don't know, just start listening within. Get quiet and listen for what's there. You will eventually hear something.

If you do decide to forgive someone without them being physically present, trust that the energy of your forgiveness will reach them. Wherever they are, they will suddenly feel warmer. They will feel as if a hint of sunlight just cracked through their soul.

They will know.

Somewhere in their unconscious, they will gather what has happened. Your act of forgiveness will be like a firefly that spreads the light far and wide.

The space within you will open up. There will no longer be this clamp over your heart. You'll be stronger. You'll remember the exotic pilgrimage. It's going to feel a little uncomfortable at first, but at the same time, you'll be healed and liberated.

⇒ *power exercise for* ⇐
FORGIVING SOMEONE ELSE

Preparing for the Exercise

Do this one in a quiet place where there are no distractions.

Sit down, either on a chair or on the floor. And if it's more comfortable for you, you can lie down on your bed instead.

Doing the Exercise

Make sure the spine is straight and your shoulders are relaxed.

Then you're ready to dive right into the exercise.

Pick someone that you need to forgive in your life. Close your eyes and imagine that this person you picked is seated before you.

On your next inhale, imagine that you are pulling the energy of love from their heart and into yours.

Then when you exhale, you want to imagine that you are sending the energy of love right back to them.

Continue to receive and give love to this person over and over again.

This exercise will help to cleanse your heart of any resentment and allow you the opportunity to finally forgive, so you can move on with your precious life!

RECEIVE WITH EVERY PARTICLE OF YOUR BEING

OVER THE YEARS, I'VE heard too many women (myself included, at one time) say that they're natural givers—so much so that they can't bear the thought of receiving anything.

The problem with operating this way is that in the long run, you lose.

A fierce woman is one who receives just as well as she gives. She understands that both processes are one and the same. She knows that by turning away favors or gifts, by never asking for help, by giving until she is depleted, she loses grasp of all the beauty inherent in her precious feminine spirit. Because giving endlessly is an unsustainable kind of deal. And if you don't allow yourself to receive from others, you deprive them the opportunity of giving from their hearts and fulfilling that part of them that wants to be of service.

Receptivity is what makes the feminine so ridiculously alluring; it's confident, but never cocky...a softening, but never a weakness. It's quiet at times, but careful never to disappear into the background.

It's a quality that is intrinsic to the moods and rhythms of woman. A goddess who leans into her receptive superpowers is in high demand. People crave the company of a receptive goddess because with her, there are no masks. She isn't striving to make everyone feel good about themselves while denying her own needs and wants in the process. This isn't about strain and struggle.

A receptive woman is an artist in dispelling illusion. She puts her weight behind what is present. And she does it with a joy and an ease that is exhilarating to watch.

When you are receptive, this means that you know how to receive with grace. You understand the power behind the softening and the surrendering. You know what it means to "make space for…"

Your body was built for exactly that. You have a womb, which makes space to receive new life. When it's time, the womb gives that life back, releasing it out into the world, just as effortlessly as it had received it.

You have a yoni, which opens with pleasure, making space to receive a lover.

And if you weren't born with a womb or a yoni, breathing into and aligning to the energies that naturally exist below your navel and in your pelvis will help you to feel into the nature of this feminine receptive power.

And all of us have a heart center that beats with so much strength, attuning us effortlessly to the qualities of love and compassion.

Don't mistake this for weakness. This is the greatest strength in existence. The receptive nature of you is what breaks down the constraints of time and space, allowing for the flow of life to assert itself at every turn.

This same power can be found in Mother Nature. Observe any single flower and you will find that it relies upon receptivity to grow. It must receive sunlight, water, and nutrients in order to blossom and develop. If it loses its ability to do these things, it will be no longer.

The same rule goes for you, too. If you shut down, if you fall into the mindset that you're not good enough to receive, then you will stop your own personal flow. You will flail your arms wildly for a while, and you will sink. A great entropy will conquer the deepest parts of your soul, and your strength will evaporate. You will feel yourself fading away. The energies that spin and whirl so wildly in you will settle back and cloud over. Layers of mist will stifle your vibrant essence.

I don't mean to get all dramatic, but *I'm telling you*. This is essential stuff, goddess sister.

Giving Zombies Finish Last

When you can't receive, you instead become the excessive giver who puts herself last. You give at the expense of everything else. Sleep, comfort, self-care, freedom. All of that gets tossed out the window, as you start to take on the posture of a total giving zombie. Dead in the spirit, almost mechanical-like, your eyes betray an empty quality.

Imagine it this way: Let's say you have all this light inside of you (which you do). And let's say that every time you give to others—whether it's money, time, energy, advice, you name it— you lose a bit of your light.

Well, the more you give, the more your light gets dimmer and dimmer, until eventually, it vanishes completely.

Now, some might argue that the amount of light in a woman is infinite.

Maybe you think you're some kind of superwoman whose light can never get turned off. And you deserve major confidence points for thinking that way, but I need to remind you of something that I'm sure you must know deep down: Giving without receiving is only half of the circle. It'll never fill you up all the way. It'll never be enough. You will always be stumbling about, incomplete, frustrated, and depleted.

Women are notorious givers and this has to stop. We're sidelining our own needs and desires to prop up everyone else. We think that by giving to those around us, we're defining who we are, we're proving our worth.

But you have nothing to prove. Slow down now, goddess. Be gentle with yourself. You're already worthy. You know this. You don't need to be defined by constantly giving. Anyhow, the soul within you defies definition of any kind. It's boundless. It's expansive, encompassing so much beauty, the bulk of which you have not yet fully realized.

Now, this doesn't mean that you have to stop giving. This doesn't mean that you shouldn't go to comfort your child at night or that you shouldn't drive to a sick friend's house with soup on a Sunday afternoon.

You can still be there for others, just not to the exclusion of yourself. Your friend might be sick, but you also might have been coming off of a seventy-hour work week. So maybe soup is out of the question that day. Maybe instead you send a text to let them know that you hope they feel better and you spend the afternoon catching up on a book or soaking in the tub.

Giving to others is a beautiful thing, but there must be balance. You must not resist your receptive nature.

When someone says something nice about your hair, receive their words with gratitude. Don't say, "Really? I just rolled out of bed. And I haven't washed it in seven weeks!" Just thank them for the compliment. Receive the kindness. You are good enough, lovable enough, worthy enough, beautiful enough, and smart enough to be complimented.

The hair might be a superficial example, but don't take something that seems shallow or unimportant for granted. There are opportunities to receive in all ways, both tiny and enormous.

Yes, there will be times when you simply cannot step out of the giving role, like when you have a baby or a small child. They rely on you to be their everything, and you must show up for them. However, this just means that you need to also stay on top of your self-care. You need to nurture your own spirit, get adequate sleep, eat healthy meals, continue to do things you enjoy, and sneak in some breaks when you need to. Motherhood is the ultimate bootcamp when it comes to refining the ways you show up for yourself while showering so much love, energy, and attention on another.

Shake off the guilt and receive love and nurturing from yourself. And this goes for all women, whether you have a child or not.

Lean into your receptive essence. Be like the flower who reaches up toward the sunlight with joyful abandon. And move your body in ways that inspire the receptive aspect of your soul out of its hiding spot.

⇥ *power exercise for* ⇤
ALLOWING YOURSELF TO RECEIVE

Preparing for the Exercise

Sit down comfortably on the floor or in a chair.

Doing the Exercise

Close your eyes.

Put both of your hands together, palms up, in your lap. Cup them in front of you, allowing the edges of the pinky fingers to touch, as if you are about to receive some sparkling treasure.

Then, focus your third eye (that area between your brows) on the empty space in your hands.

Breathe in and out, deeply through the mouth.

This exercise will connect you deeply to the power that is present in receptivity.

If you want, practice this daily for thirty days. Go for about five to ten minutes each time.

You might notice yourself feeling way stronger at the core of your being. Receptivity will marry you to the flow and power of nature. It will put you in touch with your own natural ease and ability to accept and adapt to this ever-changing universe, inside and outside of you.

ABUNDANCE IS YOUR
NATURAL STATE

—————

IT MIGHT FEEL LIKE it at times, but in truth, you are never lacking of anything.

Fulfillment already belongs to you. It is there, buried somewhere, known intimately by your true self. The self that doesn't strive or burn for more; the self that is secure and emboldened by what is.

Your true self knows that abundance is its natural state. It doesn't have to strain to fill the gaps. As far as it's concerned, there are no gaps. There is only an endless stream.

This endless stream is your birthright. It's always moving through you. It's what connects you to the power of possibility. It's what makes you aware of all that you already possess within.

The physical world around us is fleeting, transitory. It is constantly weaving in and out of form. Everything you attempt to grasp that is outside of yourself—money, things, random experiences—all of it will one day slip through your fingers like water.

So you must plug into something that will sustain and nourish you. You've got to dig deep and align yourself to the inherent abundance that you carry in you. This abundance will remind you of your power. It will show you the limitless amounts of love, joy, and potential that swirl inside of you.

The feminine form, with all of its curves and fascinations, blesses woman with the ability to naturally open her eyes to the abundance within.

With our talents for honoring the flow and surrendering to cycles, we can start to trust in our powers as creators. We can start to become more confident and fulfilled by the love, by the vision that we carry within.

This is the secret of abundance. It isn't about pretending that you have something that you don't. This isn't any of that "act as if" stuff. You already are all of this. There's no need to put on any kind of act. You're the real deal, already. *This is who you are.*

This is you, diving all the way down, below the surface, beyond what's comfortable and safe. It's you, having the audacity to look within and to fully acknowledge yourself as a powerful, all-abundant woman right now. In this moment. Not reserving it for another time. Not kidding yourself into believing that you're not ready and will be back next week when you are.

It's all about taking the initiative. In this moment. Claiming it. Not making it any more difficult than it has to be. Your intention is like a steel bond, binding all of the things you need directly to you.

You must trust that.

You must sink into that trust and forget everything else.

Here's an exercise that will help you to tap the endless stream of abundance that you carry within.

→ power exercise for ←
CLAIMING ABUNDANCE

Preparing for the Exercise

Find a quiet, comfortable place to sit or lie down.

Doing the Exercise

Focus on the base of your spine and imagine that there are roots coming from it and delving into the ground. Imagine that those roots reach many feet down under the earth, connecting you to the power of nature and cycles, connecting you to all that is.

Feel this deep and sacred connection. Breathe into it.

Say these words: "*I feel abundant. I feel fulfilled. Everything I need is inside of me.*"

Say these lines a few times, and as you speak the words, really feel it. Connect to that feeling of abundance and fulfillment within. Let yourself go there. Feel the abundant garden of possibilities and love swelling up inside of you.

This exercise will help to root you down and nurture a feeling of stability, while aligning you to the natural abundance of Mother Earth.

STRETCH THE FABRIC
OF YOUR SOUL THROUGH
YOUR STRUGGLES

———

WHEN MY MOM WAS a young girl growing up in the Philippines, her family was drowning in poverty. My mom recalls many meals in which she had to split one single banana between herself, her siblings, and her parents.

There were seven of them total.

And that one-seventh of a banana was the whole entire meal for each person. With a history overflowing with countless childhood struggles, I look at my mom and see very clearly how she rose from the pain of that time, how she summoned up all of her will and spirit to create the abundant life that she has today.

Some of the best parts of you have been born from your struggles.

Every heartache you've ever endured, every misery that has crushed your spirit like the weight of a million bricks—those are the experiences that you've needed the most.

The grief that sucked your soul dry. The injustice that silenced your voice. The emotional pain that stomped away your glow. That defeat that you suffered, the one that ripped every last shred of faith out of you.

Every woman, since the beginning of time, has known what it's like to struggle. Unconsciously, whenever we sink into the depths of our own personal pain, we are also feeling the collective pain that every past, present, and future woman has ever and will ever endure in this world. Once you become aware of that, once you deeply feel the invisible lines of energy that connect you to every woman, living or not, you will truly understand the sacred science that is your feminine power.

And you will also understand that as you rise up from the ashes of your own struggles, all other women rise up with you. The work you do of reclaiming your inherent power is not only done for you; it is also done for the sake of all women.

So you must rise. You must go beyond what is comfortable for you. Stretch the fabric of your soul. Because it can take it.

Your struggles and your failures are not your enemies. They were not meant to be forgotten, ignored, or overlooked.

If we succeeded every time we tried something, the entire world would grow lazy and uninspired. If we never tasted the bitterness of loss and heartbreak, we'd have no opportunities to develop ourselves and to truly understand the many textures of this human life.

You would never grow if your life merely consisted of sunshine and flowers. Your soul would never blossom in the ways that it desires. You must know this. Deep inside, you know. Even when you curse all of the things that keep you stuck, or you wish that you could wake up to new life circumstances tomorrow, you must know, within, that you are being offered a divine opportunity to expand into the fullness of the goddess that you are.

As far as I'm concerned, the ones who have it easy in this life, who have insulated themselves from pain, who have numbed out their relationship to emotions and deeper ways of expression—those are the ones who refuse to listen to the whispers of the soul. In doing so, these beings obstruct their flow and cut off any chances of expanding into a life of deeper meaning and purpose.

Living this way, for a woman who is deeply embodied in her feminine, would be severely hollow and unsettling. The soul's aim is to always expand, especially in the face of adversity.

Kind of like mint.

I've recently started taking up a gardening habit. I don't admit to being a genius at it, but I still go out into my garden every day. As I set up my first garden, months ago, I wondered what would survive my lack of experience. I planted many seeds—sunflowers, zucchini, tomatoes, lavender, rosemary, sage, basil, and mint.

The majority of my first-time plantings failed. I did manage to enjoy one (yes, one) stunning sunflower, as well as half a dozen zucchinis. But other than that, nothing flourished.

Nothing, except for the mint.

The mint was like some kind of badass who didn't care what everyone else was doing.

All those other plants are dying cause of their inexperienced owner? Not me. I'm here to grow, regardless.

The mint was relentless in its pursuit of expansion. It grew in every direction, crowding out the lackluster plants around it. It grew even when it suffered from a lack of water at times. It grew even when the weather conditions weren't the most ideal. It grew like it was the only thing that mattered.

As it grew, I was increasingly stunned and elated by its gumption. I would go out, almost daily, just to feel the leaves of the mint plant, hoping that some of its boldness would rub off on me somehow.

→ my power wish to ←
SUPPORT YOU IN BRAVING YOUR STRUGGLES

My wish for you is that you will take inspiration from the boldness of mint.

Expand into the powerhouse of a woman that you are, even when all the odds are screaming out against you. Even when your path is greatly obstructed. Even when the crowd's betting that you'll fail. Doesn't matter. Block all that out and keep pushing forward.

The worst that could happen is that you fail again, or you get your heart broken again, or you lose your way for a month or two. And that's okay. Those things will just reveal to you other ways to know your strength.

Let every setback shine a light and serve as the blessing in disguise that it was meant to be. Feel gratitude in your heart for what pain is teaching you right now.

→ badass self-care for ←
THE SPIRIT

Your spirit, which animates the divine power of your being, requires regular self-care. It is the part of you that's in touch with the higher power. The part of you that has its eyes open to the sacredness of all beings.

When you take time to nurture the spirit, it creates a strong foundation for all the other aspects of you to come into balance and alignment.

By staying in touch with that connection to something greater than your own individual being, you can nurture ongoing self-care of the spirit.

You know best what truly offers your spirit that divine connection. However, if you're ever looking for suggestions for something easy and accessible, turn to none other than the Ultimate Mother that is nature. When a woman goes outdoors to commune with the trees, the water, the soil, the sky, and the air, she is magically liberated. Her soul is cleansed and healed. The fullness of her essence is enhanced, as nature is the deepest kind of medicine for the spirit.

→ badass self-care ritual for ←
THE SPIRIT

Preparing for the Exercise

Go sit somewhere in nature. If you can't be outside, sit in front of a window.

Doing the Exercise

As you sit, feel the energy of all the life around you. Drink that energy in to fuel your own being. Be so completely with it that you cannot tell where you end and nature begins. Tap the dynamic and divine power of Mother Nature and feel the way that she connects to your own feminine being. As you inhale, feel her energy rushing toward you, entering you from every angle, from every pore. As you exhale, imagine you are concentrating her energy into the crown of your head.

And be sure to leave phones and tablets at home. The frequency of electronics will detract from the natural wonders of nature; you want to be as tapped in as possible!

THE LAST THING
TO REMEMBER

YOU ARE A BLESSING on this planet. Live like a woman who knows this, deep in her cells and in her heart.

This world needs you to step into the fullness of who you are. No one can hold space for this except you.

Before I started walking the path of the fierce woman, I carried all of these expectations, firmly holding on to my ideas of what things in my life should look like.

But now I bow down to the spontaneity present in each day. I take each step, surrendering to the mystery that vibrates at the core of each moment. I pour my love and energy into the people, projects, and experiences that light me up—and demand nothing in return. This doesn't mean that I'm unable to receive. It means that by asking for nothing, by releasing control of things looking a certain way, I am allowing the universe to give me exactly what my soul requires.

And there's nothing more liberating than being able to open up my arms and receive in this way.

Releasing my attachment to outcome has led me down so many exciting new roads; ones that I would have never known existed had I kept clinging to ideas of how it all should go.

I want to end on this note, so that you remember, always, that the universe is working with you. It wants you to have the experiences that will draw the light and the power of what you are to the surface. If you are clenching anywhere in your life, if you are holding too rigidly to old mindsets, ideas, and patterns, the gifts cannot come. Unclench, and you will magnetize what you need without even having to pay a conscious thought toward what it is exactly.

I'm so honored to have had you on this journey. This book was created from a deep state of love. I hope that you will take some of the exercises and fierce woman wisdom from these pages, so that you can continue to joyfully blaze down the journey that is your beautiful life.

There are no limits to you, no limits to the things that you can do. The lines that have been drawn, the barriers that have been built—these things are all illusions … and opportunities for you to gather your power, once again.

Never forget what you are.

And if you do, if you need to remember yourself again, come back to the pages of this book. Let the words draw the courageous and wild parts of you to the surface. And come back to the breath, to the spark that exists within.

So that your pure, undiluted, badass self can rise and be expressed.

Deep gratitude to you, for taking this brave expedition with me.

I'm rooting for you, goddess sister. All the way.

RECOMMENDED READING

For more tips and exercises, go to my website:
http://RhodaShapiro.com

Awakening Shakti: The Transformative
Power of the Goddesses of Yoga
by Sally Kempton

The Radiance Sutras: 112 Gateways to
the Yoga of Wonder and Delight
by Lorin Roche and Shiva Rea

Love Your Lady Landscape: Trust Your Gut,
Care for 'Down There' and Reclaim Your
Fierce and Feminine SHE-Power
by Lisa Lister

Shakti Mantras: Tapping into the
Great Goddess Energy Within
by Thomas Ashley-Farrand

Tantra: The Supreme Understanding
    by Osho

The Book of Secrets
    by Osho

The Portable Jung
    by C. G. Jung

The Complete Book of Essential
    Oils and Aromatherapy
    by Valerie Ann Worwood

Meditation As Medicine: Activate the
    Power of Your Natural Healing Force
    by Guru Dharma Singh Khalsa,
    MD, and Cameron Stauth

RESOURCES FOR WOMEN IN CRISIS

National Center on Domestic and Sexual Violence
http://www.ncdsv.org

The National Domestic Violence Hotline
800-799-SAFE (7233)

RAINN
https://www.rainn.org
The largest anti–sexual violence organization in the nation.

The National Sexual Assault Telephone Hotline
800-656-HOPE (4673)

Crisis Text Line
https://www.crisistextline.org
Free 24/7 text support for people in crisis.
Text HOME to 741741 for support.

To Write the Author

If you wish to contact the author or would like more information about this book, please write to the author in care of Llewellyn Worldwide, and we will forward your request. Both the author and publisher appreciate hearing from you and learning of your enjoyment of this book and how it has helped you. Llewellyn Worldwide cannot guarantee that every letter written to the author can be answered, but all will be forwarded. Please write to:

Rhoda Shapiro
℅ Llewellyn Worldwide
2143 Wooddale Drive
Woodbury, MN 55125.2989

Please enclose a self-addressed stamped envelope for reply, or $1.00 to cover costs. If outside the U.S.A., enclose an international postal reply coupon.